# Visions of the Future

# Visions of the Future

## An Investigation of Premonitions

Dr Keith Hearne

THE AQUARIAN PRESS

First published 1989


© Dr Keith Hearne 1989

British Library Cataloguing in Publication Data

Hearne, Keith
Visions of the future: an investigation of premonitions.
1. Premonitions, history
I. Title
133.8′6′09

ISBN 0-85030-807-0

*The Aquarian Press is part of the Thorsons Publishing Group, Wellingborough, Northamptonshire, NN8 2RQ, England*

Typeset by Harper Phototypesetters Limited, Northampton
Printed and bound in Great Britain by Mackays of Chatham PLC, Chatham, Kent


3  5  7  9  10  8  6  4

# Contents

1. Backgrounds     11
2. The Bad News     25
3. Not-so-bad News and The Good News     45
4. The Percipients     63
5. Science and Foreknowledge     78
6. Excuses and Explanations     97
7. Futures     111

*Reference List*     134
*Index*     139

This book is fondly dedicated to
Katherine and Sarah.

# Acknowledgements

I should like to extend my sincere thanks to the many hundreds of people who have supplied detailed accounts of their premonitions and completed questionnaire information for me.

I am particularly grateful to the three percipients who were grilled extensively by me for inclusion in Chapter Four of this book.

# Preface

I started investigating reported premonitions after years of arduous but not very fruitful research into seeking minute bodily-signals accompanying telepathy, using a variety of sophisticated electro-physiological techniques. That work, which was in addition to my main preoccupation with sleep and dream research, was quite fascinating but in retrospect it does seem rather too much to expect any parapsychological effects to turn up on demand in the exceedingly artificial environment of the university laboratory.

Then, one day, I experienced what may or may not have been a premonition, but which certainly excited me and generated a special interest in that area of 'psi'. Coldly and statistically, the episode could have been a coincidence, but actually to go through such a thing is perplexing and makes one suspect that, although it seems inconceivable, perhaps foreknowledge can indeed sometimes arise in certain circumstances. The true scientist must of course respond to such anomalous cases in a positive way by considering why such events might happen and by what means. Unfortunately, there is an unreasoning and unscientific bias by many academics against parapsychological research which makes progress difficult at this time. A similar strong bias from colleagues resisted my early research into 'lucid' dreaming, until the results were published and accepted.

Having become intrigued by premonitions, it did not take long to find someone else who had apparently perceived the future. The niece of a good friend had foreseen, by several hours, the massive Flixborough explosion in the UK on 1 June 1974. Believable witnesses gladly confirmed her story. Articles in newspapers on the topic produced hundreds of reports of seeming premonition. This book presents the results of my investigations into the incredible field of foreknowledge.

Keith Hearne, B.Sc., M.Sc., Ph.D.
Hearne Research Organization
PO Box 180
Hull
North Humberside
HU1 2EW

# 1

# Backgrounds

Doreen Wallis woke in a terrible state, crying uncontrollably and with sweat pouring from her. 'In my dream I was standing at my front door, looking towards the school, waiting for my daughter to come home for her dinner. I saw this small aeroplane circling the school and then it seemed to dive straight at the school. It pulled round at the last minute and crashed into an alley-way in front of me. There was nothing anyone could do.'

Doreen had to wake her husband because she was so affected by the incident. About five months later, an aircraft did just miss the school at lunchtime and crashed into some houses a little further along than in her dream.

What would you think if something like that happened to you? It would certainly make you wonder whether you had actually seen into the future, and if so you'd probably be very puzzled as to why you had been so privileged. You might even ponder upon whether you had in fact caused the later event in some inexplicable way.

What, also, if you experienced not just one but many such apparent premonitions over the years? Not surprisingly, many people in that position feel freakish and clam up, not daring to mention their occasional foreknowledge of things even to their nearest and dearest — except parapsychologists. In fact, most of the cases of premonition cited in this book are from people who report that they have had several other instances of foreknowledge.

Unfortunately, official science has assumed that premonitions are quite impossible, so there is no point in investigating cases. The situation is reminiscent of the period when many 'scientists' refused to look through Galileo's telescope at celestial phenomena which contradicted their belief system concerning the structure of the universe.

However, fortunately, a small community of parapsychologists — scientists with open minds — are prepared to accept reports of premonitions and apply scientific methods to their study.

## Definitions

Before we launch into the fascinating and awesome area of premonitions, let us first make certain of some of our basic terms so there is no puzzlement or confusion over their meaning.

In words that will not raise the hackles of some philosophers too much, we might say that a *premonition* is an experience which appears to anticipate a future event and which could not have been inferred from information available before the event.

Doreen's dream was such a case. She adds that the content of the dream and its accompanying emotion set it apart from ordinary dreaming and made a strong impression on her. The similarities between the dream and the later incident would seem to be too close to be accounted for by coincidence, bearing in mind too that Doreen has had several premonitions in her life. Of course, if after assessing the evidence we decide to reject all the 'normal' explanations of the episode, we are necessarily asserting that some very strange process, as yet unknown to science, is behind these phenomena.

The word premonition comes from the Latin *praemonere*, meaning to warn in advance. It implies that the later happenings will be unpleasant in some way, and certainly most reported cases are of that nature. They so often concern death, injury, and destruction.

The word *precognition*, meaning 'before knowing', may also be encountered. It has a more neutral flavour and is most usually applied in reports of laboratory experiments.

The person who 'receives' the premonitory information is often referred to as the *percipient*, although that term suggests that all premonitions involve a sensory element and that may not always be the state of affairs.

Parapsychologists categorize premonitions as a variety of 'psi' phenomena which include, *telepathy* (distant feeling), *clairvoyance* (clear seeing), *psychokinesis*, or PK (mind over matter), and other scientific anomalies. Those are some of their fields of study. It has been ascertained from survey work that four out of 10 of reported cases of psi involve apparently knowing the future in some way. The term PSI (the Greek letter ψ) is the modern term that has ousted 'ESP' (extra-sensory-perception) and covers telepathy, clairvoyance, precognition and psychokinesis.

Sometimes, percipients report simply having a 'feeling' (which can be very strong indeed) that something will happen but are unable to be precise as to what will take place. That type of experience is sometimes called a *presentiment*, or *foreboding*.

I would like to describe a presentiment that I experienced just a few years ago. It had such an effect on me that I changed my parapsychological research to the field of foreknowledge. I had boarded the Humber ferry one evening and sat down. At that moment I 'knew' with absolute certainty that some untoward event (I did not know precisely what) was going to take place on that trip. Words simply cannot reflect the intensity of that sense of being totally sure that it would happen. It was so powerful that I wanted to tell the ferry's Master, but I realized that there was nothing really he could have done as a result of my vague warning. I considered disembarking, but the uniqueness of the experience excited my scientific curiosity, so I sat fast.

Although I had made the crossing many times before, with no qualms whatsoever, this time I found myself looking around for anything that would float in case the vessel sank.

When the boat was some 200 metres off the other jetty, a cry of 'Man overboard!' was heard. A male passenger had fallen from the bow. It was dark by now and nothing could be seen in the water. There was no sound. After some 20 minutes of searching, the man was fortunately sighted, dragged aboard and resuscitated.

From that small experience of my own, I now understand the overwhelming feeling of *certainty* that is described by so many subjects. Actually, if something dramatic had *not* occurred on the crossing after that incredible foreboding I would have been considerably perplexed!

## Types

Premonitions have been found to emerge from four basic states:

dreams, waking imagery, waking thoughts, and a form of imagery that some people experience when falling asleep. The most frequently reported of these conditions is the dream state.

## Dreams

Dreaming is a period of internally generated imagery, predominantly of a visual kind, and is associated particularly with a period of sleep called 'REM' or rapid-eye-movement sleep. Dreaming sleep appears every 90 minutes or so after falling asleep, alternating with slow-wave-sleep (SWS). Its duration increases at each cycle in the night and the total amount of dreaming time per night may be about two hours.

REM sleep is identifiable by certain characteristics. Most of the body's muscles are in fact paralysed during dreaming sleep, except the breathing musculature and the eye muscles. Breathing is more shallow and variable than in slow wave sleep, and there are bursts of quick, jerky eye movements.

It is of interest to note that dreaming sleep has been shown to be helpful not only to premonitions, but to telepathy in some experimental researches — although other studies have not reproduced those results. Typically, the arrangement in these 'dream telepathy' experiments has consisted of a 'transmitter' person looking at pictures that have been randomly selected. This happens when the 'receiving' subject is dreaming, as confirmed in a sleep-laboratory. The dream reports obtained from the subject on being woken from dreaming are compared with the 'transmitted' pictures by independent judges. A basically similar arrangement, but where the 'transmitted' material is replaced by randomly chosen experiences that happen after waking, has also given evidence of precognition.

Dreaming sleep, then, may be of special significance to mankind in providing useful information conveyed by some mysterious means.

Premonitory dreams are said by many subjects to be outstandingly vivid. On waking, the dreamer feels that the dream was meaningful and contained an important message describing circumstances, usually unfavourable, that will shortly come into existence.

**Waking imagery**

If you ask people to envisage a scene in their mind, say the front door of their home, you will get widely different reports between them on how well the task can be performed. Some say they can conjure up a vivid, coloured image with no difficulty and even 'project' the image onto an external surface such as a wall (not of course for others to see). [1] Those are good imagers. Other people, and I am one, cannot visualize anything at all. Most peoples' imaging ability is somewhere between those extremes.

Consider for a moment that although we all use the same vocabulary, certain subjective words can have varied meanings depending on the person. The word 'daydreaming' for instance, means purely thinking to me, yet I am aware that to some people it signifies observing clear, detailed pictures generated at will. I find that ability strange to comprehend myself, but at the same time I am fully aware that individual differences are rife in human psychology so I accept that some people can visualize with ease. Similarly, we should be prepared to accept that some people perhaps have 'psychic' abilities. Any one person's own experiences do not provide adequate information by which to understand those of others.

The imaging process of wakefulness is probably the same that operates in dreams — there is no reason to expect separate systems — and some premonitions appear to percipients as daytime 'visions'.

**Sleep-onset ('borderland') imagery**

Some good visualizers, when just about to fall asleep, tend to see clear, vivid pictures. Technically, the phenomenon is known as hypnagogic imagery. Sometimes they are reported, by persons prone to foreknowledge, to have particularly reliable premonitory content.

One feature of all these types of premonition is that the information occurs spontaneously. Cold, deliberate prediction by persons who have premonitions seem to show no particular accuracy.

### In the past

If cases of premonition had only been recorded since, say 100 years ago, then considerable doubt could justifiably be cast on the whole idea of foreknowledge. However, there is ample documentary evidence to show that examples of precognition have been around throughout written history.[2] Not only precognition, but the allied areas of telepathy and clairvoyance have an equally reliable basis. These phenomena therefore have a definite permanence, which greatly increases their significance and presses more forcibly for their scientific recognition and attempts at explanation.

In all societies, great and small, there has been a belief that under certain circumstances the future could be revealed. In earlier times, as now, the dream was known to be the main source of precognition. Thus, for instance, in the great civilizations of Assyria and Babylonia, it was fully accepted that dreams could be interpreted so as to foretell events. Our knowledge of this derives from cuneiform-script clay tablets found in those areas.

The ancient Egyptians thought that dreams were messages from the gods. Certain papyri, such as the Chester Beatty papyrus (1350BC), have survived describing their beliefs. Dream incubation was practised whereby a person wanting an answer to some personal problem, or help in making a decision, would go and sleep at a special temple. The 'incubant' would, before sleep, indulge in various cleansing rituals so as to be mentally prepared for the divine communication. The temples were called Serapeums — named after Serapis, the Egyptian god of dreams. There were famous temples at Thebes and Memphis.

Dreams reported by the incubant were interpreted by the 'learned men of the magic library'. Sometimes the dreams were considered to represent warnings of dangers yet to occur. Lists have been discovered detailing dream activities and the conclusion as to whether each is a good or bad sign. For a woman to dream of being kissed by her husband was a bad sign. There was a notion of 'opposites' in dream interpretation, in that the true meaning of a dream theme was the opposite to what was observed. Thus, a dream of a birth could signify that there would soon be a death.

The Atharva-Veda is a book of wisdom from India dating from over 1000 BC. It includes the beliefs of that culture concerning the interpretation of dreams. One interesting observation was that the time of night at which a premonitory dream happened could give a rough guide as to when the actual event would take place. A dream occurring early in the night would come to fruition after a longer period than if the dream was nearer dawn.

Several thinkers in ancient Greece commented on precognition.

Aristotle stated that it is difficult either to ignore the evidence or to believe it. In his work '*On Divination*', he points out that some dreams about future illness could be caused by an unconscious appreciation of symptoms not yet noticeable (prodromic dreams). He also thought that sometimes the percipient acted unconsciously so as to bring about the fulfilment (wish fulfilment). Some dreams of the future that come true could, he believed, be explained by coincidence — and yet there remained cases that were inexplicable. He further remarked that the content of precognition-dreams is not random. They mostly concern our personal friends. [3]

In the ancient world there were no special terms for what today we call precognition, telepathy and clairvoyance. They were all forms of divination ('*mantike*'). Divination was sub-divided according to the technique by which the information was obtained i.e. 'technical', (actively) from divination of, say, entrails or by astrology, and 'natural', (passively) from dreams and altered states of consciousness. Dreams were held in special esteem as a vehicle for receiving precognitions. Plutarch stated that 'the dream is the oldest oracle'.

An anecdotal account records that Alexander the Great had a dream of a satyr dancing on a shield when he was besieging the city of Tyros. Aristander interpreted the dream as a play on words: *Sa Tyros* (Tyros is yours). Alexander did indeed capture the city after a seven month siege.

To the Greeks, though, there was a common belief that foreseen unpleasant events could be averted by sacrifice, prayer, washing, or 'telling it to the sun'.

Roman society was steeped in the belief that the future could be foreseen. Julius Caesar decided to cross the Rubicorn and attack Rome after dreaming of incest with his mother. The oracle saw this as symbolic of territorial conquest. His wife Calpurnia was supposed to have dreamed of her husband's assassination the night before it happened, according to Plutarch.

Cicero gives, among many other examples of dream premonition, the case of Simonides who found the body of a stranger on the shore and had it buried. At that time Simonides was planning to go on a sea voyage but he had a dream in which the buried man warned him not to go because the ship would be lost. Simonides did not make the journey and it was discovered later that the ship had sunk, drowning all aboard.

Prophetic dreams have had a marked effect on the development of some religions at crucial stages. There are about 15 dreams mentioned in the Old Testament, most of which occurred at critical points in history. Perhaps the most famous dream in the Bible was that of the Pharaoh who dreamed of the years of abundance, then of famine, as interpreted by Joseph.

## Scrying

One universally employed technique which could produce images of future as well as present events was that of 'scrying'. It involved gazing at something that would produce random shapes and shades. Some people, good vizualizers, can see definite pictures under such circumstances. It is a form of induced day-dream. It was accomplished in a number of ways, including the use of a shiny surface or speculum, perhaps burnished with a little oil (catoptromancy); a bowl of water to which a drop of oil has been added (hydromancy); ink poured into the palm of the seer's hand. Crystal-gazing is another version of the phenomenon. Sometimes the speculum was placed on water, but not submerged, especially at holy wells or springs. The arrangement facilitated the production of divinatory information by the influence of the 'pneuma' rising from the water.

Scrying was a part of religion. An epitaph from AD 129 describes a priest of Dionysus at Salonica as an official 'hydroscopist'.

In early times pre-pubescent boys were used as seers, not only because this imagery is probably better and more imaginative in children, but also because the seer was supposed to possess a certain purity in order to be favoured with privileged information from the gods.

The early psychic researcher F.W. Myers thought that one person in 20 could see images when scrying, and that of those perhaps one in 20 obtained information not attainable by ordinary means.

## Omens

An omen is a happening that precedes an event or behaviour and which seems to reflect unfavourably on it by way of symbolism. The ancients regarded them very seriously. There are also innumerable examples in English history;

When Edward, Duke of York (father of Edward IV) was being sworn in, in the Chamber of Peers, a crown hanging on a lighting contraption suddenly fell. At the same time apparently, a crown which stood at the top of Dover castle also fell. These incidents were taken to be omens that the royal line would change, which is what happened.

The silver cross that was carried before cardinal Wolsey fell out of its socket, striking a servant of the Bishop. A little while later Wolsey was arrested and was later beheaded for treason.

Also, the head of the staff of King Charles I fell off at his trial. The king was of course subsequently beheaded.

As a modern example of an omen from my files there is the case of 29 year-old Valerie Lister who had picked up her three children from school one day. She was walking along with another mother and her two children. A large magpie appeared seemingly from nowhere and started to attack Valerie's youngest boy, Barry, who was 4 years old. The group attempted to shoo the bird away, but it kept returning to peck at him. It was several minutes before the bird finally relented and flew off. Later that same evening, at 7 p.m., Barry walked into the road outside his house and was killed by a vehicle.

## Auguries

An augury is a form of divination based on the chance outcome of some ritualistic behaviour. There are numerous varieties including inspecting entrails, reading tea-leaves, and throwing bones. An ancient Chinese book of divination, the I Ching, is entered at a point randomly selected by the pattern of sticks that are thrown.

The name Nostradamus is often bandied about in discussions of foreknowledge, but the facts about this man and his prophecies are not so widely known. The Frenchman Michel de Nostredame (Nostradamus is the Latin form) was born in Provence in 1503.[4] He studied medicine at Montpellier and began a lifetime of seemingly dedicated caring for the sick, particularly the victims of the plague. Ironically, his first wife and her two children fell victim to that disease.

He wandered widely, at one period having to evade the infamous and paranoid Inquisitors who were unhappy about some remarks he once made concerning a statue!

Nostradamus eventually remarried, this time to a rich widow, and settled down in Salon. It was there that he began to write almanacs and his book of prophecies. Each prophecy is written in the form of a four-line verse or 'quatrain' and they are given in groups of 100 (called 'Centuries'). He intended to write 1000 quatrains but the seventh hundred is not complete, so there are in all 942.

The prophecies are not in chronological order. The first two quatrains are not prophecies but describe the divining technique. Nostradamus used a method recorded by Imblichus (a fourth century Neoplatonist), details of which had been republished in a book in 1547. A bowl of water was placed on a brass tripod and the seer stared into the water until images of the future appeared. The prophecies became very popular all over Europe and Nostradamus was given a royal audience with Catherine de Medici on three occasions. Nostradamus died in 1556.

The effects of his prognostications on history have been considerable. As one example, the Maginot line of fortification was built because of one quatrain which the then French Chief of Staff was convinced referred to an invasion of France through Switzerland. Hitler's megalomania was also encouraged, it seems, by the prophecies.

Unfortunately, on inspection, the quatrains are found to be extremely vague and open to many different interpretations. Out of the 940 prophecies almost any historical event could be made to fit, especially since they are in random order. A few quatrains do seem to refer quite well to historical episodes:

> 'Beasts wild with hunger will cross the rivers, the greater part of the battlefield will be against Hister. He will drag the leader in a cage of iron, when the child of Germany observes no law.'
> Ibid. page 90

The name Hister is similar to Hitler. Also, here:

> 'The fortress near the Thames will fall when the king is locked up inside. He will be seen in his shirt near the bridge, one facing death then barred inside the fortress.'
> Ibid. Page 360

Does this refer to Charles I, who was locked up at Windsor and executed wearing a shirt?

Those are two of the best correspondences, but most are very ambiguous and some seem to be definitely wrong. Scientifically, the predictions could not be said to be of much value. Anyone making a thousand predictions would, by chance, expect some 'hits'.

## Seventeenth-century miscellany

To take just one written account of premonitions of various kinds, from the seventeenth century, John Aubrey FRS collected accounts of strange happenings which he included in his 'Miscellanies'.[5] Among these were accounts of apparitions (some coinciding with death), poltergeists, precognition (he tells us that the astronomer Edmund Halley had a dream before he went to St Helena, of seeing the island. When he actually approached the place it was exactly as he had previously seen in the dream), and the phenomenon of seeing one's own apparition — or 'doppelgänger':

> The beautiful Lady Diana Rich, daughter of the Earl of Holland, as she was walking in her father's garden at Kensington to take the fresh air before dinner, about 11 o'clock, being then very well, met with her own apparition as in a looking glass. About a month later she died of the smallpox. It is said that her sister, the Lady Isabella Thynne, saw the like of herself before she died'.

Aubrey himself reported having experienced the 'death-rapping' phenomenon:

> Three or four days before my father died, as I was in my bed about 9 o'clock in the morning, perfectly awake, I did hear three distinct knocks on the beds-head, as if it had been with a ruler or ferula.'

A case of a visual effect preceding a death was noted:

> The Lady Viscountess Maidstone told me she saw (as it were) a fly of fire fly circle her in the darkness half an hour before her Lord died. He was killed at sea and the like before her mother-in-law the Countess of Winchelsea died.'

Aubrey gives several examples of a similar 'fiery apparition' known as the 'corpse-candle' which is a pale light seen at places where a death will soon happen. The number of lights is said to correspond to the number of fatalities, and the size of the light indicates whether the victim is a child or adult.

'. . . the Lady Comptroller of the house, going late into the chamber where the maid servants lay, saw no less than five of these lights together. It happened a while after, that the chamber being newly plaistered, and a grate of coal fire therein kindled to hasten the drying of the plaister, that five of the maid servants went to bed as they were wont (but as it fell out) too soon; for in the morning they were all dead, being suffocated in their sleep with the steam of the new tempered lime and coal. This was at Langathen in Carmarthenshire.'

That account was supplied to Aubrey by one J. Davis in 1656. Aubrey cites this from a German informant:

'In Germany when one is to die out of one's family, or some friends, there will sometimes likewise happen some token that signifieth the death of one e.g. some (or one) in the house heareth the noise, as if a meal-sack fell down from on high upon the boards of the chamber; they presently go up hither, where they thought it was done, and find nothing; but all things in order.'

A notable premonitory dream of the early nineteenth century concerned the assassination of the then Prime Minister Mr Spencer Perceval. The dream was recorded by Cornishman John Williams, a mines Superintendant from Redruth:[6]

'About the 2nd or 3rd day of May, 1812, I dreamed that I was in the lobby of the House of Commons (a place well known to me). A small man, dressed in a blue coat and white waistcoat, entered and immediately I saw a person whom I had observed on my first entrance, dressed in a snuff-coloured coat with metal buttons, take a pistol from under his coat and present it at the little man above mentioned. The pistol was discharged, and the ball entered under the left breast of the person at whom it was directed. I saw the blood issue from the place where the ball had struck him, his countenance instantly altered, and he fell to the ground. Upon inquiry who the sufferer might be I was informed that he was the Chancellor of the Exchequer. I understood him to be Mr Perceval, who was the Chancellor of the Exchequer (and Prime Minister). I further saw the murderer laid hold of by several of the gentlemen in the room.

'Upon waking, I told the particulars above related to my wife; she treated the matter lightly and desired me to go to sleep, saying it was only a dream. I soon fell asleep again, and again the dream presented itself with precisely the same circumstances. After waking a second time, and stating the matter again to my wife, she only repeated her request that I would compose myself and dismiss the subject from my mind. Upon my falling asleep the third time, the same dream, without any alteration, was repeated, and I awoke as on the former occasions in great agitation. So much alarmed and impressed was I with the circumstances above related that I felt much doubt whether it was not my duty to take a journey to London and communicate upon the subject with the party principally concerned. Upon this point I consulted with some friends whom I met on business at the Godolphin mine on the following day. They dissuaded me from my purpose, saying I might expose myself to contempt and vexation, or be taken as a fanatic. Upon this I said no more, but anxiously watched the newspapers every morning as the post arrived.

'On the evening of the 13th May, my second son returning from Truro, came in a hurried manner into the room where I was sitting and exclaimed, "Oh father, your dream has come true. Mr Perceval has been shot in the lobby of the House of Commons." '

Mr Perceval was shot on 11 May, 1812, some eight or nine days after the series of dreams happened to John Williams. The assassin was John Bellingham, who was later hanged. Years later, in 1876, Mr C.R. Fox, the son of the one of the persons told about the dream, confirmed the account.

As an example of a well-attested premonition in fairly recent history, concerning a momentous event, there is the case of Bishop Joseph de Lanyi's foreknowledge of the assassination of Archduke Ferdinand and his wife Sophie at Sarajevo. The Bishop, a former spiritual adviser to the couple, had a dream at 3.30 a.m. on the morning of 28 June 1914 in which he received a letter having a black seal and bearing the Archduke's motif. On the letterhead was a scene showing the assassination in a motor vehicle, and the letter from the Archduke stated that he and his wife would be killed the next day.

The Bishop told his dream that morning to some witnesses, and then held a special Mass for the victims. Later that day the murders really happened. The Archduke was the heir to the Austro-Hungarian throne and the assassination was instrumental in starting the First World War.[7]

In this chapter the terminology applied to premonitions has been elucidated and it has been established that satisfactory evidence exists that premonitions have been continually chronicled throughout history. In fact, bearing in mind the long-standing nature of the phenomenon of premonition, it becomes clearly remarkable that the area has not been subjected to the degree of scientific interest that would inevitably have been focused on any other anomalous events so reliably and consistently reported for millennia. Possible reasons for this worrying neglect will be considered later in this book.

The next stage of this exploration of foreknowledge will be to observe a reasonable selection of modern cases in order to determine the themes of foreknowledge and the persons referred to in them. This will provide a suitable data base of modern cases.

# 2

# The Bad News

When accounts of premonitions are broken down into categories, it is found that the most frequently reported type of case concerns death. Death happening to immediate members of the family is the theme of many reports. Babies and children figure prominently.

'I have experienced many premonitions. One was when I was six months pregnant with my second baby. I had a vivid dream where the baby was born by Caesarian, that it was a boy, and it only lived 18 hours. When he died he was in a plastic box lined with white flowers.
'I did have a boy by Caesarian, and he lived for 17½ hours. When the doctor told me he had died I couldn't cry, so they took me down to see my baby. He was dressed in a nighty, surrounded by white chrysanthemums laying inside the incubator just as I dreamt.'
JEAN DAVIS.

'I had a dream that my sister's baby died and of the funeral that followed. The dream was very, very, vivid, so much so that when I woke up I cried to my mother about it. Four days later my brother waited for me to come home from work to tell me my sister's baby had died in the early hours. It was established that it was a cot death. She had choked on vomit in her sleep.'
B. BALL.

The foreknowledge can extend to adopted children:

'We adopted a baby boy whom we called Graham. I had several premonitions about him. Seven years after we had adopted him, at Christmas, I had a strong conviction that it would be the last one with Graham. One Saturday, the next month, I was putting Graham's clothes out for him when it came into my head to put out his brightest clothes which could ward off danger. It seemed silly at the time because he was only going to play in the garden. That day I was unusually calm. Later that morning one of Graham's friends called to play. They asked if they could go to the playpark. I let them go, it was close by with no main roads to cross.

'As they went I watched them go down the road, then it came into my head, this is the only way I can put it, 'You will not see Graham alive again.' My hand was on the window catch to call him back, but I could not open the window. My hand would not move.

'Later, a policeman came to take us to the hospital. Graham had been knocked down by a car. He died three days later after being on life support. He was killed on a stretch of road I had felt danger for him when he was a baby.'
R. SMITH.

There are cases where children experience premonitions. In this next case the victim was the young percipient's brother:

'The first of my very many premonitions came to me when I was eight years old. As my mother was getting ready my five year old brother, Teddy, to go out, I heard my own voice tell me, 'Teddy's leg will be squashed.' I was afraid to tell my mother. She was very strict and would have told me not to 'tell stories'.

'An hour later on our way to visit my Grandmother, my little brother was knocked down by an army lorry and because of his injuries his leg was amputated. He died six months later.'
HILDA BROWN.

'When I was 12 I dreamed of seeing a cousin shoot himself accidentally while going over a stone wall when hunting wild duck. In the morning I told my mother and she said it was only a dream. I was frightened though, and also told my teacher when I got to school; but nobody took any notice of me. On going home from school I was met by my father and realized something was wrong. He said my young cousin had accidentally shot and killed himself today out after wild duck. I was frightened of my dreams for a long time afterwards.'
SHIRLEY CARVER.

Adult victims are the most prominent though in accounts of foreknowledge:

'I had a very vivid dream, in colour. I was holding a new born baby girl with blonde hair. Then I saw Nigel, my second son, coming towards me arms outstretched. In waking life he was perfectly well and getting on well in his profession, but in the dream he looked deathly. His face was drawn and skeletal, his body wasted. He was holding his lower abdomen as though in great pain. 'I have been killed', he said. At that juncture he pointed to a field where a chestnut horse stood by a gated fence. The next morning I was about to tell the dream to my daughter, but she reminded me that 'Friday's dream on Saturday told will come true however old.' However, I told her on the Sunday morning.

That evening my daughter informed me that she was pregnant. Her blonde baby girl was six weeks old when my son, Nigel, died. Nigel moved into a new bungalow six months before he died and the rural scene was exactly as in my dream. At the end of the road was a wooded field with a gated fence. I took my granddaughter to see the chestnut horse that stood there.'
BETTY CORICA.

'I was planning to travel with my two children to join my husband in West Africa. The night before the flight I had a very bad dream in which my husband, a deep-sea diver, was drowning. Two months later my husband did drown in a diving accident, just as I had dreamed — in every detail. It shook me to have seen the future.'
S. BALE.

'I was having a happy dream of enjoying myself at a crowded party, when suddenly I was reading my sister's death insertion in the paper. Her full name and address were right before my eyes. Three months later, to the day, my 28 year old sister Brenda was electrocuted. This was my first experience of having a dream come true.'
MARY MCBRIDE.

A New Zealand woman provided an example of a waking vision of a person who died shortly afterwards:

'I have small premonitions all the time. A few years ago though I 'saw' my father-in-law who was living in Holland, 12,000 miles away. It was in broad daylight. I came in from the garden and he was standing by the sink. I was not surprised or frightened. I spoke to him but he did not answer. He just looked sad, shook his head and was gone. A month later he was dead. I knew full well that my vision indicated that I wouldn't see him alive again.'
JUDITH DITZEL.

The premonitory message may keep appearing, as if urgently warning someone to take avoiding action:

'I had a recurring dream every night for a week. In the dream my mother, who was dead in reality, paid a visit and told me, 'You will not see Doug and Joy again. They will not be here long.' Doug and Joy were my brother and his wife.

'The dream was very disquieting and I wanted to warn my brother, but my husband told me not to be 'silly'. Two days after I last had the dream I bought the local paper and on the front page were my brother and Joy. They had been killed in a Dan-Air plane crash flying to Spain. I had no idea they had gone on holiday.

'Another curious thing is that my other brother, Peter, also had a premonition. He took them to the airport and even told Doug he didn't want him to fly.'
M. COOKE.

In some reports, the precise date of a death is indicated:

'I dreamed that a local undertaker came to our cottage door in Essex. He had a plank of wood with him and gave me a bill with a date on it.

'A month later my husband died on the date given in the dream and the bill for the funeral was the amount previously shown.'
ANICE SUTTON-SHAW.

'I have had many dreams of death. When my sister-in-law was taken ill I saw in a flash a date and said to my daugher, Jill, that her aunt René would die on the 18th of the month, in 10 days time. I dreaded the day coming, but it did, and René died precisely on that day.'
JESSICA MARTIN.

'I had a dream that my beloved mother was going to die on the 10th July. I was so upset that I told my husband. I could not settle knowing what I had dreamt and so I told my mum.

'My mother laughed a little, trying to make me feel better. She said, 'It could be five or six years from now.' In fact, my mother did die on 10th July that year.'
MARJORIE WOOD.

Marjorie has experienced several other premonitions of death, and two more are worth relating:

'In a dream I saw my uncle in a taxicab. The next thing I knew, my uncle had been crushed to death inside the taxi. Two weeks later I did something unusual. I switched on the TV and watched 'Calendar', a local news programme. Within a minute it showed a railway line and gave out the news that my uncle, the one in my dream, had been killed on the line. I went to pieces and dashed into a neighbour's home.'

'My brother had just become a father for the fifth time. In my dream he informed me that his baby had died. Two weeks later my brother and his wife came to tell us that my nephew had died unexpectedly.'

Foreknowledge also extends to cover the death of friends, colleagues and acquaintances:

'The following premonition has stuck in my mind because I feel I could have, and should have, told my friend and perhaps she would still be alive. I had grown up with my friend but we hadn't seen much of each other since we had both married, and not at all in the two years before my dream.

'In my dream she came to see me and told me that she had a lump in her breast. It was removed in the dream but she was told she could only expect to live another 18 months to two years. In the dream she died and I was in the woods near to where we live. There were her mother and father, her husband, and one bunch of daffodils. They were sprinkling something on the ground.

'Five months later my friend did actually come to see me, in tears, and told me that a lump had been found in her breast. My friend underwent surgery and she battled against cancer for 19 months, but then succumbed.

'I was terribly upset and could not go to the funeral. Another friend's mother said she would make up a wreath and as she lived near the funeral place, would leave it there for me.

'There were loads of people and flowers at the cremation. Later, her ashes were scattered in a wood where she always walked her dog. Her husband had picked out my wreath, out of all of them, to place it on the ground by the ashes as they were her favourite flowers — daffodils!'
JEAN DAVIS.

In the next case the percipient recalled his premonition at a crucial point and took a course of action that may well have saved his life:

'I woke up bathed in perspiration. It was a long time since I'd had such a vivid and detailed dream. I had dreamed of being in a plane that made a rough landing and then burst into flames. People had been killed. I was going on a business trip in three days' time to China. Ought I to tell my colleagues? Did they have a right to know? After much agonizing thought, I decided against telling them.

'By a string of seemingly random events, I found myself changing seats with a colleague, Eric, when it came to the actual flight. I then discovered that I was sitting in the same position as in my dream. The plane reached Athens airport and started to land. The plane veered off the runway and careered through the perimeter fence in a way identical to the way it happened in the dream. I could feel the pilot pumping the brakes and found myself pressing down on the floor in sympathy, but the plane fell down a steep slope and stopped. Looking through the cabin window I saw the flicker of flames. Thick, deadly smoke was beginning to fill the cabin.

'Although the nearest exit was towards the rear, I remembered my dream. Now I knew I had to go forwards more than twice as far as to the rear exit. I did so and managed to jump out of the door, slightly injuring myself in the 15ft fall. People at the back of the plane however were trapped. Of the 142 passengers, 14 had perished and of the six persons in Row 25 (my original seat row) five had died, including my colleague Eric.'
GUY STAFFORD.

Persons barely known to the percipient may sometimes feature in premonitions:

'I woke one morning with a feeling of unease. Having ascertained that all was well with the household, I was absorbed by our morning routine. It was after my husband had left for the office and while the children and I sat at the breakfast table, that I knew that the problem lay with a friend, Joan.

'I could not credit the *certainty* I felt. I telephoned her to tell her of my unease but to my horror and her amazement she told me that the news of her mother's death had been communicated to her a little earlier.'
KATHLEEN MILLS.

'I was shopping in a store one day, when I picked up a black jumper. I *knew* at that moment, with absolute certainty, that I was going to wear black at a funeral. I had no feeling of dread and knew that the death was not going to upset me too much. Then came my error. I started to apply reasoning to the premonition. The only person who fitted the bill was my grandmother who was in her late eighties and was becoming more and more sad and frail as the years went by.

'In fact, a few people known to me died over the next few months, including a neighbour's son and a friend of the family, yet I knew certainly that these did not fit the premonition.

'Then a programmer who worked for me, Brian, spent the afternoon phoning car rental companies. He wanted to hire a van to drive to Bath, his home town, to collect his belongings. On the Saturday I read the local paper and there it was; the police were trying to identify the driver of a white van who had crashed into a bridge, killing himself.

'On the Monday morning my boss appeared in the computer room. He had a serious expression on his face. Before he could speak, I said, 'It *was* him.'

'As Brian's immediate superior, I represented the company at the funeral. And so I found myself, two days before Christmas, wearing black at a funeral of a lad I barely knew.'
H. DANIEL.

'I was in the sixth form at school when I had the first of many, many experiences of seeing unpleasant events in advance. There was a boy in my form whom I didn't know well and he had a younger brother also in the school. The younger brother was about 13. One night, I had a dreadful nightmare in which I was crossing the nearby Lough in a sailing boat with the younger boy. The boat capsized. As it sank I extracted myself from the ropes and rigging, but I could see the young boy struggling to free himself. I tried to free him but was unable to do so. I awoke with a terrible sense of doom and fear.

'During the day I met a friend, a lecturer at the university, who was a colleague of the boy's father and told her of the nightmare. That evening she phoned me to tell me that the same young boy had apparently tried to cross the Lough that day in bad weather (he was apparently a good helmsman) and his boat had capsized. The boy drowned.'
ROSEMARY WHITE.

The victim in premonitions may even be quite unknown to the percipient:

'My husband comes from Manchester and he liked to visit for weekends whenever possible. On one occasion I felt very nervous about travelling. On the Wednesday night I had a very vivid dream which really upset me. I saw someone lying in the road after an accident, a female with long blonde hair. I was blonde, but I didn't have the same long hair. I was however convinced it was me.

'We went to Manchester that weekend and I forgot all about the dream. Normally we would have started back on Sunday morning but we decided to go to the swimming baths near my sister's home that morning.

'We parked the car and, as we were saying goodbye, a little girl with blonde hair ran from behind our parked car into the path of an oncoming car. She died. As she lay in the road my dream came true. I felt I might have caused the dreadful accident just by having the dream.'
MARION THREADGOLD.

The next case was a really remarkable premonition:

'I went with my sister to Germany for a two-week stay with my niece and her husband who lived in married quarters. There was to be a party but, the night before, I had a dream. All the furniture had been arranged along the walls. A couple came in and asked if I had heard of the accident at the camp that morning. Three soldiers had been killed. The dream was so vivid that I asked if such news had been mentioned the previous night, but it had not.

'That night we arrived for the party. The room was exactly as I had seen it, we sat down for a drink and the same couple came in. I knew straight away what would happen. They said the very words that I had heard in my dream. My niece, her husband, and my sister looked at me open-mouthed. "You mentioned that this morning!" they said.'
M. ELLIS.

Occasionally, although the victim in a premonition seems to be clearly identifiable, the actual event befalls someone else, but linked in some way to the apparent victim. It is a 'displacement effect':

'My husband is a crane driver. He sometimes has to travel along the main road. One night I dreamed that he had a terrible accident. I did not say anything to him about the dream, but I was glad to see him home in the evening.

'A week afterwards, the police were at my door telling me my 20 year old son had been killed in a road accident in Germany.'
SHIRLEY CARVER.

'In my dream, I was at a swimming pool trying to resuscitate a baby which had drowned. I did not succeed and I asked a doctor who was there for help. After that I woke feeling devastated and told my husband about it.

'Later that same day, in the evening, two policemen called. They told me that our 21 year old son had accidentally drowned in a

swimming pool after a game of water-polo at university, where he was a student. The life-guard and the doctor, who were there almost immediately, failed to revive him.'
E. HERMAN.

'I woke distressed believing that the events of my dream had really taken place. I dreamed that my closest friend had drowned in the Thames in an old paddle steamer. Some weeks later I learned that another close friend (with the same name, Barry) had drowned in his bath due to an epileptic fit. This link struck me quite forcibly.'
DAVID COTTAM.

'I experienced a dream in which I was a disembodied onlooker, watching a car speeding down a road towards a roundabout. In the middle of which my son Gary was playing. I knew with horrible certainty that Gary was going to die on the roundabout. The car came to a sudden stop then disappeared and, to my relief, my son was sitting on the pavement rubbing a small knock on his leg. A few weeks later another Gary, whose existence I knew of through a friend, was killed close to a roundabout. In addition, on the day of the accident, my son Gary was roller-skating outside our house and sustained a minor graze to his leg.'
MARY GILL.

Some premonitions concern people in the public eye. There were very many reported cases of foreknowledge of the assassination of President John F. Kennedy of the USA. The shooting, supposedly by Lee Harvey Oswald, happened on 22 November 1963 while Kennedy and his wife Jacqueline were being driven in an open limousine at Dallas, Texas.

'Of all my premonitions, the one about the assassination of President Kennedy was the most outstanding. On the Tuesday before his assassination I had just put my daughter to bed and had a cup of tea and a quiet sit down before starting our evening meal. I wasn't thinking of anything in particular when I actually 'saw' in my mind's eye the whole episode of the shooting. I even saw it in colour. It was as if I was a spectator in the front row.
'His car had just passed me. There was much cheering and President Kennedy was smiling and waving. Suddenly he slumped forwards. People were running towards his car but security men were keeping them back. I came to, and didn't really know why I'd thought it. Three

days later, when the pictures came on TV, it was exactly, to virtually the last detail, my day-dream.'
NORMA HARVEY-PLEWS.


'I had a premonition the day before the shooting of Kennedy. I dreamt that I was watching a plane land and when it landed a great crowd of people were rushing about shouting "The President's dead!"

'Later that evening I was watching TV, when Richard Baker's face followed a Newsflash caption. I immediately knew what he was going to say and although President Kennedy was only reported as injured at that stage, I knew he was dead. I found this absolutely unnerving.'
KAY WILKINSON.


'I was watching TV one evening on my own, with my husband and son in the next room. I saw a Newsflash on the screen and then an announcement declared that President Kennedy had been shot. I told my husband and son and we sat back and waited for the main news programme. There was nothing about it, and the morning newspapers carried no story about it either. So, thinking I was going bananas, I forgot about it. But the next week, to the day, the assassination really happened.'
B. KAY.


One woman had a peculiar premonition, of the 'media announcement type',* which may have given spurious credence to the 'Russian Plot' theory of the assassination:

'The day President Kennedy was murdered my husband and I were travelling by car to an RAF base in Norfolk, England. At about 11:45 a.m. we were passing through a village when I noticed a newspaper placard stating PRESIDENT KENNEDY ASSASSINATED. I shouted, "Stop! Stop! Kennedy is dead!", but my husband could not stop at that moment and we passed on.

'We went on looking for another newsagents. At Buckingham I asked people at a cafe and at two newsagents about the news but no one knew about it. I began to feel foolish. When I arrived at the base I asked my daughter, but she too had not heard anything. In fact, the assassination did not happen until several hours after I had seen the placard.'
MARION SIMPSON.

*See Chapter 5.

Half an hour before Kennedy was shot, a mysterious phone call was received by the *Cambridge Evening News*. The anonymous caller told a news desk reporter that if they contacted the US embassy a major story would be available. The CIA mission in London informed Washington of the call, and a memo reached J. Edgar Hoover, the FBI chief. The memo helped to propagate the idea of a widespread conspiracy involved in the act, and some right-wing journalists suggested that the KGB were behind the phone call.

The fact is though that in that same geographical location two people who were convinced that Kennedy was dead were asking others about the news. It seems a more likely explanation that someone who thought that their local paper had been slow off the mark, because of the apparent placard further back along the route, telephoned a sarcastic message.

The first man to orbit the earth in a spacecraft was the Russian cosmonaut Yuri Gagarin, in October 1975. Years later he featured in a strange premonition happening to the next subject:

'I have had many premonitions throughout my life. In one I was walking along a dark road and there was an open field nearby. I looked towards the sky and I saw something falling from it. Thinking it might be a falling star I went into the field to look, after hearing the thud of it crashing.

'It seemed to be a tiny baby about six inches long. I took it to a house and washed the dirt from it. It had a man's head and face. It was the face of Yuri Gagarin. Two days later it was announced that he had been killed in a plane crash.'
MARGARET HULL.

The so-called 'Yorkshire Ripper' who was frequently murdering women in the 1970s caused widespread fear in the north of England. One woman had a near-accurate dream about one of the victims:

'I went to a supermarket and heard a man speak with a northern accent. It started me thinking. I went home and was in the middle of a recipe when I noticed a story about the 'Ripper' in a Sunday newspaper.

'I then had a premonition of a girl with dark hair, in dark jeans, walking along near a supermarket. I could see a man jump out from near a wall and hit her on the back of her head. I 'saw' him dragging her along. I could see he had black curly hair like a gypsy. I could see a wire mesh fence and little pebbles on the dark soil, and stark twigs.

'I detected that the girl's name was 'Jackie Hall'. I could not see the lower half of the murderer's face as he seemed to be wearing a dark balaclava or mask. I heard a tune which kept going through my mind. It was 'Bridge Over Troubled Water'. This was apparently the favourite tune of the girl who was the Ripper's 13th victim, Jacqueline Hill.'
SYLVIA AVINS.

As a footnote it should be mentioned that very many people, including Sylvia, stated that they knew when the Ripper's arrest was imminent.

British Parliamentarian Airey Neave, shadow Secretary for Northern Ireland, was assassinated by the IRA in 1979:

'During a period of six months I had several premonitions in the form of dreams. In one I was watching myself as I poured over the many pages of obituaries in my usual paper. I recall seeing the name Airey Neave. There was also a vehicle, a motor-car, in one of the pictures. I told my common-law wife about the premonition the following morning and sure enough, later that day, he was blown up in his car at the House of Commons.'
PAUL FINCH.

An American percipient informed me:

'I have had premonitions for a long time. As one example, I was walking in a bus station in Delaware when I received information and mental pictures over a period of about five seconds. I knew that a young man would get off a plane from Hawaii, go to New York, and shoot John Lennon at night in front of his apartment building. He would be in the middle, with his wife on the left and the assassin on the right. I 'saw' this happening from across the street and from above. I also saw the subsequent candle-lit procession just as it appeared on TV.'
N. MEIER.

People have been known to act on a premonition and in so doing avoid being involved in severe accidents. The following subject states that he has had many 'unexplained premonitions'. One in particular was remarkable:

'After having completed my apprenticeship as an aircraft engineer. I left London to work in the Midlands with a light aircraft maintenance company. One of my duties was to fly as Observer on air tests, with our Managing Director as pilot. Air testing can be dangerous, as the aircraft is taken to its limits such as stalling, spins and single-engine climbs.

'At first I enjoyed the thrill of flying but I soon became dogged by a recurring dream of being sat in the right-hand seat attempting to pilot the aircraft with my boss sat next to me, unconscious. The problem was that I could not fly the plane.

'After a while, the dream began to haunt me every time I got into a plane to carry out an air test until one day my nerve went and I refused to fly.

The next air test crashed, killing both the Managing Director and the apprentice.'
PHILIP LAMMIMAN.

The next percipient believes that she saved her father's life because of a premonitory dream:

'Just before I got married I dreamed that my father, who was an electrician and also drove cranes for British Rail, was climbing up a metal stairway to reach a crane when half-way up there was a terrible flash of lightning and he fell down dead.

That morning I woke up just as my father was rushing off to work. I refused to let him go until I warned him of a fuse-box which I had seen in my dream. He laughed, but when he returned home from work at lunchtime he said that a thunderstorm in the night had caused the fuse box to become live. He told me I had saved his life, and he hugged me tight'.
D. HALL.

Louisa Rhine gave this American case:

'During the war my husband was in command of a Naval ship, and naturally thoughts of him were often in my mind. After he had been away for almost two years I dreamed one night that he started home by plane. The plane was wrecked and everyone aboard killed. I had that dream on 14 consecutive nights. I wrote telling him that when he returned, if it were humanely possible, not to come by plane. Several months passed and early one morning he called me from California airport saying he had just arrived and would leave in about an hour. He asked me to meet him in Washington the following day. I was horror stricken. My feelings are difficult to describe, but I felt he must not fly. I persuaded him to come by train. He cancelled his reservation and had coffee with several officers who had flown with him, and turned in for a few hours sleep. When he got up he found the plane on which he was to have left had crashed about 10 minutes after it left the field and everyone aboard was killed.'[1]

Sometimes, an unconscious influence appears to affect the body psychosomatically so resulting in avoiding action:

'In the war I was in the fire service. On one occasion we were on our way to a school in Abbey Road where reinforcements were required. We approached the area, but I had a terrible feeling of suffocation and sickness.

'We were near an ARP station, so we stopped off to see if I could get a drink of water. An air-raid was on at the time. We then went to Abbey Road. As we turned into it, we saw the space where the school had been. It had just had a direct hit. Had we not stopped off, we would have been killed.'
JOAN HAWTHORN.

In the next case, the percipient simply could not understand why she felt compelled to behave so rudely to a friend, but it might well have been because she was responding to a strong premonition and was attempting to avoid the event:

'I had received a letter from a very close friend, Audrey, who was returning to England after several years in the USA. I was thrilled at the thought of meeting her again, and I asked for a day off work. I met Audrey in Liverpool and she was keen to wander around looking at the shops and have lunch at Henderson's before going to my home at Waterloo.

'We walked a few yards, then suddenly the kerbstones and pavement flags seemed to yell at me to go my own way and let her go hers. This is the only way I can describe the experience. I couldn't understand it at all, but I had to leave her somehow or other. It was a feeling that something dreadful would happen if we stayed together. All I could imagine was perhaps a bus or lorry crashing into us both, whereas if we parted we should be all right.

'Not being able to explain this to my friend, I lied to her, telling her that I was very sorry but I had to go into the office as something urgent had cropped up. I said I would meet her later. She was disappointed, but then left me saying she'd wander around before going to Henderson's.

'My boss was surprised to see me and, as it turned out, there was urgent work to do. My boss went out. Later, he returned and said that there has been a big fire in the city centre. I learned a little later that it was at Henderson's.

'My blood ran cold. It still does when I remember. I spent the rest of the afternoon in a state of extreme anxiety, wondering what happend to my friend. At about 4.30 p.m. Audrey arrived at the office. She was white and shaking with nerves. She said that after leaving me she'd walked around the streets and then decided to eat at a cafe in Bold Street. She had then walked down to Henderson's and arrived there at the precise moment a man had jumped from the flames at the top of Henderson's, and had obviously been killed. She'd also seen others follow suit.'

GWEN COLLINGWOOD.

A rather similar case is reported by Louisa Rhine, concerning an American girl:

'When I was newly married I got homesick one day. I just had to go home. Billy fussed a little, but gave in to me and ordered the one and only taxi to take me to the morning train. I remember how joyful I was and how I danced about the house waiting for the taxi. Billy and the driver teased me, but I was too happy to care. Just as he bought the ticket cold fear gripped me. I started to cry. 'Give him back the tickets', I said, 'Please, Billy, we can't go on this train.' Billy went into one of his rages, but the ticket man reached out and took the tickets. 'Do as she says. Always do as she says.' We got into the taxi and all the way to the hotel they asked me why. I did not know. I just cried. At dinner that night there was a commotion. The taxi man was coming towards me, pushing people to one side and upsetting chairs. he cried, 'How did you know not to go on that train? It wrecked at the next town. The car you always ride in turned over and everyone was killed.'[2]

In the next case, a premonition sensitized a mother to a dangerous situation and her son's life was saved:

'I had a dream about my two year old son, Benjamin. I was looking into a hollow where there was some water with thick weed and saw my son's shoes at the side of the bank. I knew he was somewhere under the weed, but my sister and my husband were looking for him. I was frantically running to and fro, somehow knowing we wouldn't find him.

'About six weeks later my sister visited with her children and suggested that we all went to Cleethorpes. We went to a sandpit by a boating lake. The children were playing nicely in the sandpit until

Peter and Ben decided to climb the steps. We were sat pouring orange when it all went quiet.

'I stood up and asked where Ben was. I walked to the top of the sandpit and saw a hollow with water, full of weed. I started to run and Peter was running towards us. We knew by his face that Ben was somewhere in the water.

'When we got near the edge he was about two feet under. My sister was nearest to him and she pulled him out. We were lucky; he was OK. All I could say as I was shaking him by the feet was "The dream I told you about the water; the weed!" Everything was true.'
CHERIE RILEY.

Disasters and accidents that reach the headlines are foreseen by some percipients:

'I had just got off the bus in London's Whitehall, carrying groceries, and en route to my office in the National Liberal Club. As I turned the corner into Whitehall Place, it was clear that there had been some kind of explosion; people were lying on the pavement, with others bending over them. There was a lot of broken glass and blood.

'The blast appeared to have come from the left. Everyone was clustered on the right as though thrown or blown that way and the windows on each side of the opening of Scotland Place on the left were the only ones that still had glass in them.

'I couldn't understand why nobody in Whitehall had reacted to this, or why I hadn't heard the explosion. I then realized that there was no sound at all; no screams and no traffic noise. The scene was quite silent, as though a screen had slammed down behind me. Then normal sounds resumed and the 'vision' disappeared slowly.

'I staggered into the office for a strong coffee, feeling as shaken as if it had been real. The following day, when a rail strike prevented me from going to work, the IRA bomb went off in Great Scotland Yard just round the corner from where I had the premonition. The army recruiting office was bombed, together with the Old Bailey courts. One person died and 238 were injured.'
PENNY HOPKINS.

On 13 January 1982, a Boeing 737 airliner, taking off from Washington DC in snow and freezing conditions, could not gain height and crashed into the Potomac river. The disaster was made vivid to people because TV cameras showed some desperate and courageous attempts by rescuers to reach survivors floundering in the river. 78 passengers and crew died. Only five people aboard the plane lived. It was an event that was referred to in several accounts of foreknowledge:

'I went to the front door to let my dog in one afternoon. I had a picture imprinted in my head of a plane. Everything was white and I was straining my eyes to see. I kept being shown the wings of a plane.

'I had such a strong feeling of disaster than when my husband came in for tea I told him immediately and also informed a friend. I kept saying, "It's all white. I can't see and I'm going to crash!"

'That night news of the plane crash in Washington came through. What hurts most is not getting enough information to stop these things happening.'
JUNE LAWRENCE.

'I observed the same plane crash in a dream a week before it actually occurred, and then again three days before the event. I told my daughter that this dream was different from any other dream I ever had. I saw a plane crash into a bridge, and water. I saw the people, but I did not know where or when it would happen. When I saw the pictures on TV I cried because I thought I should have been able to help; especially the girl in the water.'
MARIE O'CONNOR.

The worst plane crash in history happened on the ground at Tenerife airport on 27 March 1977. In thick fog, a KLM Boeing 747 taking off struck a taxi-ing Pan Am Boeing 747. The total number of people killed in the disaster was 582.

'I woke one morning in a state of panic. I must have screamed out, as my husband sat up in bed startled. He asked me what was the matter. I told him that two massive aircraft had crashed, but not in the sky. I was stood almost underneath one of the planes and people were screaming at me to help them. I *knew* it was at Tenerife airport, on the ground.

'I told a few friends about my dream. Seven days later it happened. I cried so much because I kept thinking what I could have done to avoid this terrible disaster.'
V. SUMNER.

'I had been awakened from a dream in the early morning and saw a head-on collision between two aeroplanes. One was landing, the other taking off. I was horrified.

'Later, at lunch time, a Newsflash came on TV.'
DOLORES BROWN.

On 28 February 1978, a Northern Line underground train in London crashed into the buffers at Moorgate station. There were 41 deaths and more than 50 were badly injured:

'I heard of the disaster, in which a lot of people were killed, 24 hours before it happened, on the radio. I asked at work about it and thought it very strange that no one else had heard it.

'Well, I heard the same item again the next morning. I just couldn't believe it. I thought about it for quite some time, and I wondered if maybe a relative of mine might have been on the train.'
D. SAXTON.

On Friday 4 March 1987, the ferryship *Herald of Free Enterprise*, owned by Townsend-Thoresen, sailed with its bow doors open. Water inundated the vessel and it capsized just outside Zeebrugge harbour, Belgium. 189 people died in the disaster.

'For some months before the event I had occasional 'pictures in the mind' of a ferry on its side in water. The images were vivid and the ferry was 'seen' to be bright red. I even reasoned that it was one belonging to the Townsend-Thoresen company.

'In the week before the disaster the episodes of imagery increased steadily in frequency and on the actual day I became extremely anxious and uneasy, sensing the imminent event.

'Suddenly, at 5:45 p.m. my mood changed and a feeling of resignation came over me. I now knew that the event was inevitable. I watched the early evening news on TV but there was no mention of a ferry disaster. This was puzzling to me because of my very great conviction that something had happened. However, later that evening when the capsize was reported, I was overwhelmed with emotion, felt sick and sobbed. I shall never forget how I felt and I never want to experience it again.'
ANN KITCHING.

Apart from these premonitions, which involve some kind of perception or thought of an actual event, some accounts consist of a sort of symbolic indicator of an imminent happening:

'I was coming home one evening when the man who lived next door came in just after me (we lived in a maisonette). I happened to turn

round to speak to him, but all I could see was black. It was as if he was surrounded by a black cloud and I could not even see his face properly, although he was standing quite close to me. It was five days later that this man had an accident and died.
K. FLETCHER.

'One evening, five weeks before my boy-friend died suddenly and unexpectedly, I saw very many lights (like fairy lights) around his head and shoulders. I was standing about six feet away from him and the lights suddenly went as I approached. I could not understand what they were, and I was greatly intrigued. I had not seen such a thing before, nor have I since.'
BOBBI GARDNER.

Apart from such visual effects sometimes preceding death, several mysterious noise phenomena have been linked with death. A physicist reports some personal examples:

'I was in my bedroom reading, when there was a formidable "crack" from a wooden shelf holding my books. I thought the wood had split but the shelf was undamaged and very solid. I could have stood on it. The following evening another tremendous crack came from the shelf which again, on inspection, was quite firm. Two days later my father died suddenly and unexpectedly of a cerebral haemorrhage.

'On another occasion I was sitting at my bench in the laboratory when a bookcase gave a loud crack. This was followed a few seconds later by a much louder sound. I could not account for the sounds. Two days later a report appeared in the newspaper about a plane crash which killed a former colleague of mine who had worked at the same bench. In fact, his initials were still on a drawer.'
PETER JONES.

'The night before my mother died there were three great knocks at her front door at 11 p.m. The next door neighbour told me this. The neighbour thought it was her own door and went to see, but no one was there. While she stood looking there were three more knocks at my mother's door.

'My mother was in bed and heard them, but she told the neighbour the next day "I knew what they were. It was my deceased husband calling for me." The neighbour was puzzled. Later that same day my mother died suddenly of a coronary heart attack.'
OLWYN FENN.

A further variety of anomalous events that occur before death concerns clocks and watches. There are reliable reports that these instruments have stopped or started unaccountably at, or shortly before, the death of someone.

'A few minutes before my grandfather died, a clock that was in an upstairs room chimed many times. It was impossible. The clock had no weights and had been there for years without working.'
BRENDA MORGAN.

A mysterious 'ticking' sound has been found to presage death sometimes:

'The first time I heard it it was in the house but I could not trace the sound. Then, one evening, I was on the telephone to a friend, Irene. I mentioned the ticking to her and she wondered whether it might indicate an imminent passing. I felt reluctant to end the phone conversation with her and we talked until 2 a.m.! A few hours later Irene, who was only in her 40s, died suddenly of a heart attack. The ticking stopped. Since then I have heard the ticking for three more periods and each time a death occurred to someone within a week or so.'
JENNIFER DOUSE.

In summary, there are a number of different ways in which unanticipated death is sometimes inexplicably prior-indicated. The 'victim' in premonitions of death is often someone in the family of the percipient, but it could also be someone hardly known or completely unknown. Apart from the various forms of 'internally experienced' premonitions, altered perceptions and external physical effects can also give warning of approaching death.

Foreknowledge, however, also refers to other unexpected events apart from death, and these will be described in the next chapter.

# 3

# Not-so-bad News and the Good News

On a lesser scale of seriousness than the cases encountered in the previous chapter, another substantial group of premonitions covers accidents, injuries, and generally unpleasant happenings. There are also many 'neutral' premonitions of fairly trivial future events. In addition, a small fraction of cases provide positive, beneficial information with pleasant consequences!

When cases of unpleasant premonitions are broken down into categories, a strong bond of sensitivity in mothers for their sons becomes obvious. Many cases are reported by mothers who knew that an accident was about to befall a son:

'I was machining one Sunday when I suddenly experienced waking imagery. Very clearly, I saw my 20 year old son being wheeled on a hospital stretcher. I could only see his face and there was no injury that I could see. I was terribly upset by this and was very relieved when he arrived home for his lunch safely. He was intending to go out during the evening but to my relief he decided to stay in and watch TV. All the while I was very conscious of every thing he did.

The next day he had to go to Norfolk for his firm. After he had gone I could not settle and kept going into his room and doing jobs he needed doing. I switched on the radio and heard that there had been a bad accident which was holding up both lanes of traffic on the A11. I knew at once it was my son, but tried to put it out of my mind. Soon afterwards I forced myself to go to work but felt dreadful all the time I was there.

'I arrived home at 3 p.m. At the same time my husband arrived home and told me that our son was in a Cambridge hospital with internal injuries. It had been his accident that I had heard during the morning

and the police had informed my husband's firm earlier, but the message had not reached him. We went directly to the hospital. Our son was in the intensive care unit. He had no outward signs of injuries at all. I am pleased to say he eventually made a complete recovery.'
V. DUNKLING.

'I dreamed one night that my eldest son ran across the road while I was watching, and was knocked down by an oncoming lorry. This was May or June. I woke up screaming and told my husband. He thought it was a nightmare, but to me it seemed different. Anyway, in August that year my son Stephen went to get an ice-cream from a van that had stopped opposite our house. My husband and I stood by our gate watching him. We saw him run across. Suddenly a butcher's van came up the road and hit him as in my dream. Then I recalled that I'd dreamed it and that his leg would be injured. It was'.
ELIZABETH DAWKINS.

This woman had another premonition about her other son, Peter.

'I had one of my dreams. It was that my younger son, Peter, had a motor bike accident and in my dream I saw him lying in the road. That dream was on a Sunday night. I told my husband, but because of the previous dream I recalled my dream to a work colleague.
   'On the Tuesday morning, my son set off to work on his moped, full of the joys of spring, at 8.50 a.m. I was due to go to work that morning and just after 9 a.m. I went to the shops. A neighbour saw me and stopped his lorry. He said he thought Peter had been in an accident at the traffic lights. When I arrived, there lay Peter as I had seen him in my dreams. Although shocked and horrified, I did not react as if it was unexpected.
ELIZABETH DAWKINS.

'One day I was standing at the sink washing up when I suddenly knew my son was going to have an accident in his car, but I was sure he would be all right. I looked at the clock and it was 7.15 p.m. He telephoned later in the evening to say that he had an accident but was not hurt nor were the people in the other car. I asked him what time it happened and he said 7.20 p.m.'
M. STRATFORD.

In the next case, a childhood recurring vision was remarkably similar to a situation that arose later in the person's life. It was a sort of premonitory ghost.

'As a little girl I had visions. I saw a little red-haired boy inching his bottom along the pavement as he was unable to walk. His left hand hung limp and useless, and his left arm was thin and bent. His body leaned over slightly to the right. I felt sympathy for this boy and wondered who he was.

'My first son was born a spastic, paralysed down his left side and unable to walk until he wore surgical boots and a caliper, when he was nearly four. This was the child I had previously "seen" from the back view so long before his actual birth.'
GWENDOLINE CLINTON.

An element of displacement perhaps is present in the following example, in that the victim was wrongly portrayed.

'Over the past 10 years I have experienced several premonitory dreams. In one there was a river flowing gently, and I went and sat by it. Then I saw a child in a red dress floating face down in the river coming towards me. I did not pull the child out, but suddenly it was on the bank and all right. I told my husband in the morning.

'About a week later we went for Sunday lunch to some friends in the country; my husband and I and two sons aged four and 10. My youngest son went over to a lake with two other children and my friend's husband. We were sitting in a car chatting when I turned to the lake and saw my friend's husband dragging our son out of the water. My son was wearing a light red anorak. We rushed him back to my friend's house and put him in a warm bath. I yelled out that I had dreamed it would happen.'
RUTH BROWN.

There were some impressive cases of women knowing when their husbands were about to have an accident. The tremendous sense of utter certainty is clear in the next two cases:

'Last year I was in the lounge watching TV at about 4 p.m. with the children. An ambulance or police car went past the house with the siren going. At that moment I *knew* my husband was involved in an accident. For 5–10 minutes I sat, and then walked around, but the feeling got stronger. I then phoned his school and they said he had left 10 minutes ago. After 20 minutes I phoned the police and asked them if there had been an accident. They said yes, but it wasn't my husband. But the feeling was still there. About an hour had passed now and I was frantic. Then the police pulled up outside the house. My husband had been involved in a separate accident approximately five

minutes *after* I had phoned them. The car was squashed in completely down the driver's side and he was lucky to be alive.'
G. CHAMBERLAIN.

'I was going to meet my husband at the child clinic. On our way to meet him an ambulance roared through the town, lights blazing. My little boy asked me where the ambulance was going. I replied, before I could think, that it was going to pick up daddy. The ambulance came past again on its return and I felt even more convinced. I went to the clinic, didn't wait for him, and went in. The telephone rang. I told them the phone call was for me and that it was the hospital. They were amazed. My husband had collapsed on the way to meet me.'
MYRTLE SMITH.

It is not certain how much precognition was present in that case, it may have been simultaneous telepathy, but it is nevertheless a compelling account.

'I had only been married a few weeks when I had a very vivid dream in which a policeman came up to me and said "Mrs Threadgold? Your husband Raymond . . ." In the dream I just ran away from the policeman. I didn't want to hear what he had to say. I was expecting it to be something awful. I really worried about the dream.
   Two weeks later I answered a knock on the door and a policeman standing at the door said those same words to me as in the dream. I slammed the door. I didn't want to hear what he was going to tell me. The policeman called to me through the door, "It's all right Mrs Threadgold, your husband has broken his leg playing football. Will you go to the hospital?" '
MARION THREADGOLD.

'I know the difference between a dream and a premonition because it wakes me and I have seen it as though it has just taken place. My latest was a few months ago. I saw my husband having a stroke. His mouth was twisted, as was his arm. He was kneeling and calling to me from the upstairs landing. The shock woke me up. This came true three weeks ago, although the stroke was not quite as bad as I had envisaged.'
ELIZABETH ASKEW.

'Many premonitions have happened to me over the years. One time I *knew* that if my husband went to work one particular day he would have an accident. He did have an accident and was brought home by ambulance with a broken leg.'
MARGARET MACKENDER.

Unpleasant things happening to parents constitute a proportion of premonitions:

'One of my premonitions was that I *knew* my mother would be brought home to my house after being taken ill at work. In the car, which would be a red mini, would be a man wearing glasses and he would be the driver. Also, there would be a lady in the front passenger seat. My mother would be lying down on the back seat. This came true exactly as I had seen it.'
K. GASKELL.

'I was 13 when I experienced my first premonition. I was at school and I remember thinking to myself that something awful was going to happen to my dad. He worked for a shipbuilding company testing engines. I went home on my bike at lunchtime and I saw a man coming towards me. Although I'd never seen this man before I knew he was coming to tell my mother that something had happened to dad. The man got off his bike and came through our gate. He told my mum that there had been an accident at work. The engine my dad had been testing had blown up and he was badly burned on his face and hands. We didn't know until several days later whether he would live or not, but thankfully he pulled through.'
SUSAN EDDOWES.

'I went to see my father, who was a little unwell. I had a feeling about the stairs and I told him several times to be careful of them. The next day I visited again, only to find the glass at the foot of the stairs boarded up and blood all around. A stranger took me home. I was very upset. My husband phoned the hospital. My father had collapsed at the top of the stairs and fallen backwards. His head had gone through the window. He was lucky to be alive.'
MARJORIE WOOD.

Other relatives and friends figure in foreknowledge of unhappy events, but on a smaller scale:

'I dreamed that my sister had her baby and the nurses were trying to put the baby back as it was too young to be born. As it turned out the baby was born three months early at 3 lb 5oz but had I not phoned my sister at a certain time I feel the baby might have died. I managed to get her to hospital and they were able to give her drugs to mature the baby's lungs before the birth. My sister went into labour several times before the birth and on one occasion I had terrible sympathy

pains while sitting beside her, although she felt nothing at the time.'
ELEANOR ROUTH.

'I had a premonition about my cousin Roy who lives in Bolton. I thought it was strange to dream of him as I do not often see him. I dreamed he was riding along a main road and a coal lorry shot out of a side road and Roy was badly injured because he could not avoid running into the side of the lorry. I told my mother of the dream but asked her not to mention it to my aunt (Roy's mother) in case it worried her.

We did not see my aunt for several weeks and were puzzled as to why. When she finally came she said she had not been because Roy had been in hospital. My dream came true in every detail, and I think it was about three weeks after my dream that it happened.'
SUSAN COTTON.

'Two close friends were going abroad for two weeks, as they always did each year. They always visited me two days before setting off. This particular time I announced that I wished they were not going, although I could not explain my feeling. Two weeks later the son and daughter walked up the path to ask if we had heard from them. A few hours later we heard that they had been in a horrific accident in Belgium and to this day the husband is still partially paralysed.'

'When I was 17 I started having waking visions which came true. I knew a man called Matthew Blake, I kept seeing him have a car accident. The car was a white Allegro and the accident happened on a hill. There were trees and bushes around. The same images appeared for about two months until one day I felt extremely calm. All the irritable feeling had gone. That evening my boyfriend came to pick me up. As I got in the car I sensed something and said "I think you'd better tell me what happened." He looked surprised and told me that the night before he heard a crash and went to see. There were two cars and seven people involved. "Was one of them a white Allegro?" I asked. He went pale and answered "Yes".

'A few days later my mother was reading the local paper when she suddenly said "You know a Matthew Blake don't you? His car was in an accident." It turned out to be the car crash that my boyfriend had reported.'
GILLIAN LOCK.

'I suddenly had a premonition that something awful had happened in the family of a friend of mine, Tom, whom I had not seen for several months. So clear was the impression that I telephoned his office in London and spoke to his partner. He told me Tom was in Hastings for the day on business. I told his partner of my presentiment and asked him if he knew of any unfortunate occurrence in Tom's family. He said he had seen Tom that morning and he seemed happy enough.

The next day, Tom telephoned me in a shaken state to confirm the fact and contents of my call. At the time that I had telephoned, a coach in which his daughter was travelling had left the road and crashed down an embankment rendering her unconscious for several hours. Although Tom is a friend of longstanding, I really hardly knew his daughter.

'I also dreamed of a man whom I had not seen or heard of for 10 years or more and who was then only a casual acquaintance who lived 60 miles away. In fact I had almost certainly forgotten him. One night I dreamt of him. I was actually telling my wife at breakfast of my dream so vivid was it, and I had not actually completed telling the story when the postman arrived and there in an unknown handwriting was a letter from this very man asking if I would act for him in a professional capacity concerning a property near my home.'
PETER FAIRFIELD.

As with premonitions of death, some 'unpleasant event' cases are focused on strangers:

'One of my premonitions was concerned with a young girl who worked for the same firm as myself. I saw the girl walking down the roadway leading to the factory gates when a van belonging to the firm passed her and the back door flew open hitting her in the face. Several stitches were needed. This did actually happen a few weeks later exactly as I had seen it and to the person in the premonition.'
K. GASKELL.

'My first premonition happened at the age of 14. I was going down the road to post a letter for my mother. Suddenly, just as I had left the path of the house, a "voice" kept saying in my ear "you're going to see an accident." I had three roads to go along before I reached the post-box. The one by the post-box was a main road. I was upset by the voice. As I put the letter in the box a motor bike came up and skidded in the road. The rider came off and the handlebar went into his neck. He lay there unconscious at my feet. I ran to a nearby doctor's house, gave the news, and then went home.'
MABEL ISACKE.

'I had a vivid dream of a road accident where a pedestrian was hit by a car. To my amazement he went up in the air at the moment of impact. I'd always thought that people were knocked down. A crowd gathered and it seemed ages before help was sought. So vivid was the dream that it bothered me a lot and I wondered why I'd had the dream.

Three days later I was rounding a corner in a car with my husband and a friend when there was a screech of brakes, a bang, and a young man went into the air *exactly* as I'd dreamt it. This time I knew exactly what to do and ran immediately to the phone box. When I came out my husband was holding his head. Blood was trickling from his ears and a crowd had gathered.'
CELIA JACKSON.

'It was approximately 7 a.m. one morning when I was awoken by a large explosion outside my parent's hosue in Northolt. I turned to look at the window and could see the glow of flames outside. I got out of bed and opened the curtains to see absolutely nothing but the morning traffic as usual. I went downstairs and saw both my parents in the kitchen and asked them if they had heard the explosion. They looked at me in disbelief and said I must have been dreaming. Looking back I suppose I was until I got out of bed. I put the incident behind me and thought no more of it until two days later when I was woken by a large explosion at 3 a.m. I turned to the window and again saw the glow of fire outside. This time it was real. Looking outside I saw that a car had careered into a lamp-post and the fuel tank had exploded. Only the quick thinking of a neighbour who dragged the driver from the burning wreckage saved his life. At this point it suddenly dawned on me that this was what I had seen in my dream two days earlier. My knees went to jelly and I was overcome with a feeling of nausea.'
PHILIP LAMMIMAN.

Untoward future events involving oneself are also the topic of some reports:

'In the RAF I flew on bomber raids over Germany. In May 1942 I had a strange premonition that I would not return from the next raid. In my mind (not a dream) I "saw" myself floating down over enemy territory. There was an intense fire and the blazing bomber hurtled down and smashed into a village, completely destroying a pub. The premonition was so intense that I sorted out my personal papers, etc. Our plane was hit over Holland. We baled out when it burst into flames and it hurtled away into the darkness. I floated serenely down to the ground.

'We never knew what happened to the bomber until recently. After

obtaining the German statements of the gun crew who shot us down, I have been in touch with a chap in Holland who lived 50 yards from where the burning plane crashed. It completely demolished the pub in the village of Elsloo. He has sent maps and photographs of the rebuilt pub and even parts of the aircraft he still has as souvenirs.'
LESLIE READ.

'Just before the last war I was working at a firm in the Great West Road. I lived a few miles away from the factory and cycled to and fro. I had a vivid dream one night in which I was cycling home after working overtime when an air raid warning sounded. There was the sound of aircraft overhead and a lot of AA fire. At this time I had reached the South Ealing Road and I decided to take cover. I parked my bike at the kerbside and took shelter in the doorway of a shop. Within minutes a shower of shrapnel was dropping all over the road. The raid passed and I went on home.

'Some months after the war started my dream was enacted in real life. Once again, I was cycling home late when the warning sounded. Once again, I parked my bike at the same spot in the same road, dived into the same doorway for cover and heard shrapnel dropping all around; one of the pieces hitting the handlebar of my bicycle. There is no doubt in my mind that I had a preview of the future.'
K. RANDALL.

'When I was a student at Birmingham University I went to a function at the university one night with some of my flatmates. We met other friends there and one of them offered us a lift home in his car at the end of the evening. We lived about a mile from the university and I protested that we could easily walk. I had the strongest feeling that we should not get into the car. But I knew the driver well, had been a passenger in his car many times, and he had not been drinking. But as it was a cold night my flatmates were keen to accept the lift and I did not protest any further, in spite of my strong wish not to get into the car. We were nearly home when another car pulled out of a side road, hit the car we were in, and caused an accident. I was the only person hurt, I ended up in hospital with facial injuries which have left permanent scars and slight disability.'
JENNY WICKHAM.

'I have always had strong instincts about people and situations. I had this premonition while driving to work one morning. It was 8 a.m. and I had completed about five miles of my 14 mile journey to Sidcup. I suddenly had the premonition that I was going to be in a dangerous situation. I further *knew* that this danger was to occur between the 2nd and 4th roundabouts on my journey.

'I was approaching the 4th roundabout and was beginning to think it was just vivid imagination on my part when coming towards me, three abreast, was a red sports car overtaking a lorry which in turn was overtaking another lorry. There was no room for me; my road was completely blocked. I stayed calm and pulled into the kerb and waited. The sheer panic on the face of the driver of the sports car before he eventually pulled in front of the lorry through the space I had created was awesome. He wasn't to know that it was a premonition that saved his life, and mine too. When I reflected on the incident afterwards I wondered why I had not even attempted to get out of my car, but subconsciously I had known that I would not be in personal danger.'
SHEILA EUSTACE.

'I was driving to work along the A143 towards Great Yarmouth. The morning was dry and clear, with very good visibility. I was approaching a fairly sharp bend that swept downhill to the left. There were high hedges and houses on the nearside so that the bend had to be taken blind and I normally slowed to about 30 m.p.h. to go round it. Above the hedges and between the houses I suddenly became aware of the top of an enormous truck coming up the hill and nearing the bend from the opposite direction. Thinking there would be little room on the road, I slowed down and got ready to stop if necessary. However, as I carefully edged round the bend there was no truck to be seen, in fact there were no other vehicles at all. But what was there was an old lady crossing the road with her dog. Had I gone round at my normal speed I would most certainly have either hit her or crashed the car to avoid her.'
ROBIN BENDER.

'I was living with my husband and four children in Bangkok, Thailand. My eldest son was returning to England to school and I arranged to take him and his younger brother on a river trip. On the morning of the expedition I awoke with a feeling of impending disaster. So strong was the feeling that I left my handbag and jewellery at home because I was convinced that we would come to grief on the river. We can all swim so I didn't fear drowning.

'We returned safely from the trip but the feeling of disaster remained. In the afternoon I had to go to the Embassy and the feeling was so strong that I insisted on taking my son with me. We crossed the road and waited on the road island for the lights to change. As I stepped out into the road I was knocked down by a truck driving on the wrong

side of the road. I came round in hospital with numerous injuries and an overwhelming sense of relief.'
JANET COLLINS.

'Another premonition happened to me when I was driving with my husband. We were going to town when I told him he had to slow down. I could not give a reason but in my mind I could see a tree across the road further ahead. A few yards ahead a fellow was swinging a light in the road and stopped us to redirect us. There was a tree across the road.'
SYLVIA HOLLAND.

'In my dream I was inside a school in Grimsby when a policeman appeared. he said that my vehicle had just been involved in an accident. I went outside and saw that a car had collided with the rear of my Dormobile. I told the policeman that I was clearly not at fault as my vehicle was stationary. I then awoke.

Twenty minutes later a car trying to park behind my Dormobile van, in which I was sleeping, knocked against the rear of the vehicle.'
ROBIN FURMAN.

The perplexing condition of feeling that something unpleasant might happen, but not being able to explain to others one's reluctance to enter a situation that could be hazardous, sometimes crops up. A Canadian woman wrote to me:

'I have had premonitions from the age of seven. As just one example, my brother had bought a Volkswagen. The first time he asked me if I would like to go with him for an evening out next weekend I found myself avoiding the question. I could not understand why I wasn't saying yes. I wanted to go. I just said something like "maybe". This went on the same every day that week. On the evening, I just wasn't getting ready. Before my brother went out he asked, "Are you coming?" I said, "No, I'm going to wash my hair." I knew I had no intention of washing my hair. I felt totally confused. I went to bed later and woke after a while. Almost instantly the thought was in my head: the phone will ring, it's John; he's in hospital. I wasn't frightened. The very next instant the phone rang. My father answered it. He said to my mother, "It's John. He's in hospital, but he's all right. He's had an accident in the car." He had fractured his wrist. However, we finally learned that the passenger door had had to be replaced and most damage to the car was where the passenger (myself) would have been sitting.'
PATRICIA LOMAX.

Rather more broadly, some premonitions are about situations which have some relevance to the percipient:

'I am a chartered civil engineer working for a construction company. One evening I was watching the TV news when I suddenly got a "vision" of a tunnel, three quarters filled with an inrush of gravel. At the time I was involved with a contract to modernize an old tunnel. I became so disturbed that I travelled the 12 miles to the site to see how the night shift was progressing. All was well. The next afternoon there was an inrush of gravel into the tunnel filling it up to the three quarters level at the point of inrush and tapering to some 30 metres along the tunnel in both directions. Fortunately, the gravel that was swept into the tunnel choked any more material from entering.'
GEOFFREY RICHARDS.

'I have had many experiences of foreknowledge. One was when my aged parents lived in a bungalow at the fork of two roads. I dreamed a vehicle hurtled uncontrollably down the road, couldn't make the corner nearby, and crashed through their wall, smashing and churning up the flowers and lawn. This dream occurred every night for a week.

'My father, being very proud of his rose garden, spent a lot of time there. I asked him not to go out to do any gardening, never mentioning the dream. I didn't see my parents for a week, and imagine my horror when I visited them next time to see the devastation I had seen in my dream. A vehicle had gone straight through the wall and over the garden and lawn.'
E. JACKSON.

'We were setting off on a short car trip when I suddenly had an image of a car wheel spinning off into the road. It was the near-side wheel. Our car was white, but the one in my vision was black. 20 minutes later we saw a maroon car on the verge in a country road. One of its wheels was spinning and approaching from behind. I have never before or since in thousands of miles of motoring miles seen a wheel spinning in the wake of a car!'
VIVIENNE COOMBE.

Displacement is seen in some accident premonitions:

'My son acquired a motor bike when he was 16. One night I awoke crying and told my husband about an awful dream I had. In it I could see (at that time, I thought) my son in a motor cycle accident. I could see his blue and white bike and blue crash helmet. There were trees in the road. It was a very severe accident and he lost part of his foot. Obviously I was upset, but my son was not told of the dream.

'At this time my son had a friend who had a yellow and white motor cycle and orange helmet. About a fortnight later we came home from shopping to find two identical bikes in the drive and two blue crash helmets. The next week my son's friend had an accident in a tree-lined road and lost his foot and part of his leg.'
LYNNE MORRISSEY.

Sometimes people report having had a recurring premonition for many years before the event actually happens:

'From the age of about five years until I was about 30, I had a dream at least once every two or three weeks about being in a field with an aircraft crashing, or about to crash, and parachutes above me. I was always afraid and awoke crying. All my family and friends knew about this dream. About 10 years ago I was in this field (the field in the dream) when two jets collided above me. The parachutes were there and I was crying but it was because my dream had come true and I just couldn't believe it. No one was killed. I was in no way involved with anyone with the planes. I have never had the dream since.'
ANNETTE OSBORNE.

The next account is an unusual one, of a shared recurring premonitory dream.

'My mother lived in a very lonely place where there were only two cottages, so she had my aunt to stay with her to keep her company as my father was away to war. One morning my mother said "I've had an awful dream. I dreamt that a man came late at night to ask if we needed a sewing machine mended." "That's funny", said my aunt, "I've dreamed the same dream".

'Next night my mother dreamt the same dream, so did my aunt. The third night they both had the same dream again. Mother said that we must get prepared in case something happened. "We must pretend there's a man in the house in case somebody comes along", she said.

'On the fourth night, when it was pitch dark, a knocking, came on the door, mother said to my aunt, "Who will go out first to the door?" My aunt led the way with an old-fashioned lamp (they had no electricity). Standing at the door with his foot inside the threshold was a man. "I've come to see if you have a sewing machine", he said. My mother said to my aunt, "Get Elijah with the gun, quick!" The man

ran off, thinking my father was at home. The police came looking
around several times but nobody was about.'
MRS JACOBS.

Fairly innocuous incidents appear in some accounts. Probably
they are more common than are reported because they are not
considered to be so interesting by percipients:

'I was 20 years old and had just begun a new job as an assistant librarian
in Newcastle. I dreamt that a Dutchman came into the library to ask
about some Dutch language novels. In the dream I went to the file
where such requests were kept and could not find it, but eventually
tracked it down in the back room where another assistant was dealing
with it.
    The next day it did happen. The Dutchman came in about his
request for Dutch novels. Instead of searching the file I went straight
to my friend in the back room, who was indeed working on that request
then. It was a few minutes before I realized that what had happened
was a premonition. Then I felt quite alarmed.'
SUSAN TOWNSEND.

'One of my premonitions was funny. I woke up in the middle of the
night and could hear a tapping on the window. When I looked, I
could see a Red Indian in his war outfit — feathers and war paint and
a chopper in his hand. I knew I must be dreaming and I was laughing.
Next morning I went to work and told my pal about it. I was expecting her to laugh but instead she went white. I asked her if she was OK.
Then she took out of her handbag a postcard she had received that
morning from her friend in Canada. On the front was a photo of a
Red Indian just as I've described. Her friend's name was the same as
mine and the letter ended "Love, Dawn".'
DAWN STEWART.

'My premonitory experiments are simple ones. I used to hear the
telephone ringing before it actually was. Also, I always used to move
to pick up my crying daughter a full minutes before she actually started
crying in another room. My husband used to get annoyed. He thought
I made her cry.'
LORNA SURYA.

Hidden among the doom and gloom of the great majority of
premonitions are a small number which give prior knowledge of
advantageous, profitable events:

'In the early hours of the morning I had a dream of someone telling me a horse was going to win, and its name was BEAN something. Over breakfast I asked my husband if he had heard of a horse by that name. He said he hadn't, and we joked about it because I have never had a dream about a horse winning and I am hopeless at picking a winner at anything. My husband sent my son to get the daily paper. My husband said he couldn't see a horse of that name listed.

'As I sat down for a coffee at 10.30 a.m. I grabbed the paper and straight away I saw the horse listed — BEAN BOY. I was so excited I rang my mother, my sister, my brother-in-law, and a friend, Harry, who likes a little flutter. They each placed a £1 bet on the horse. We put £20 of the mortgage money on it. The horse won (at 7 to 1). I was thrilled.'
MARION THREADGOLD.

'I dreamed I was at work on my machine and a man came to me to tell me I had won on the pools. He handed me a cheque but did not come right up to me. He handed it to me over the conveyer belt, causing me to turn my head and take my eyes off my work. The cheque was for £88 and I felt disappointed.

'The next morning I filled in a coupon at work and also told a girl working with me about my dream. We both laughed about it and she asked if that was the reason I was filling in the coupon. I had not done the pools for many weeks before the dream. I checked my coupon and found that I had 8 draws, but there were 14 draws that week. I received £256. I received the cheque the following Friday and stitched a staple through my finger accidentally in the afternoon.'
MARIE MELLOR.

'My eldest son lost his signet ring while throwing snowballs in the front garden. He was very upset because his financée had given it to him. During that night I had a dream that I could see the snow had melted under a rose bush by the front gate and there was his ring shining in the sunlight. Next morning I hurriedly went to the rose bush by the gate and there was the ring just as I had seen it in my dream. I have also dreamed of the names of racehorses winning big races prior to the event, not even knowing the horses even existed. Last year I dreamed the winner of the Grand National. My family were very grateful and cashed in on my dream!'
BEATRICE VENN.

'My daughter had a dream in which her father said "Look into the third drawer of the locker". My husband passed away suddenly last year

and money was very tight. We both looked but nothing was there. About a week later I was in the bedroom and I don't know why, but I opened the fourth drawer and as I moved a paperback book inside, I could not believe my eyes, for there was £210 in £10 notes.'
VIOLET JOYCE.

'My husband and I were in a cinema and during the interval I told him he would have a small win on the football pools and told him the amount of money he would actually win. The following Thursday he received a cheque for exactly the amount I had predicted.'
EILEEN BARBER.

'My husband and I used to be competition dancers. I would often dream about forthcoming events. For instance, my husband and I had been placed 2nd and 3rd a few times but had never won. I dreamed that we were given number 22 and that it was a Latin American competition and that we won. I waited six months. Eventually we were given number 22 and it was a Latin American competition. I knew that we would win, and we did. I also dreamed that my friends were number 46 and they won. The night they were given 46 I said to them that they would win. They just laughed and didn't believe me. They won.'
DOROTHY HUGHES.

'I am often aware of things before they happen. On one occassion I woke and told my husband that I had dreamt that a horse called "Golden" something had won the 3 p.m. race at Sandown Park. I had young twins at that time and seldom had time to read a newspaper, and I am ignorant of anything to do with horse racing. My husband was intrigued by my dream and said we should check the runners. As it happened it was one of those days when the newspaper was not delivered. We forgot all about it until we watched TV and saw that a horse called "Golden Rod" had unexpectedly won the 3 p.m. race. My husband's name is Rodney, but everyone calls him "Rod".'
ANNE KENYON.

'A few years ago I had a mental picture of a race course with tall trees either side. I saw the horses running and heard the names of the first and second places loud and clear over a speaker; "Val's Girl" and "Juliette Marney". At this time I had no knowledge of horse racing, so I asked around the family about the trees either side of the course. The race turned out to be the Oaks, but the bookmakers had not yet got a list of runners as the event was a long way off.

'As the time neared, there they were listed. Of course the family started placing ante-post bets along with a few friends who got to hear of my premonition. I was quite nervous by the time of the race. However the order of winning was reversed. "Juliette Marney" won and "Val's Girl" was second.

'Imagine my surprise when my slip was taken in — the bookmaker paid me in error "Val's Girl" 1st, "Juliette Marney" 2nd. So, for me at least, the premonition was correct!'
GILLIAN WHATNALL.

Sometimes a symbol or sign is recognized in a dream that indicates an imminent event, either pleasant or unpleasant:

'My husband owned and trained some racehorses, working particularly hard with one called "Turk". I always knew when it would win because I would dream of eating cream buns or the like, and perhaps also of being in the presence of royalty.'
IRENE FURMAN.

'If I dreamed of coal or fire in any way, it always preceded getting a windfall soon afterwards in real life.'
PHYLLIS SCOTT-CLARK.

'It all started some years ago when three nights running I dreamed of a white wedding dress. Seven to 10 days later three people who I was friendly with passed away. It has happened many times since then. Whenever I see a white wedding dress in a dream, someone I know or knew passes away.'
MARGARET JACKSON.

The phenomenon of *déjà vu* ('already seen') is like a forgotten premonition but it is only recalled when the event is about to happen. Thus, a person going to a place they have not visited before suddenly realizes that it is somehow familiar and may even be able to accurately predict what is round the next corner; or they may know precisely what is going to be said next in a conversation:

'I have always had a sense of déjà vu as long as I can remember, and have always known things even though I couldn't possibly have. For example, when I was about 22 I visited a friend who had just moved in-to a new flat. She said "You must see the painting Paul (her boyfriend) has given me as a wedding present." I said that she'd already shown it to me. She said she couldn't have done as he'd only given it to her

just before we arrived. My husband, who was with me, asked me to describe it. I did so and my friend said it was nothing like the painting. She went and fetched it and it was exactly as I had described, except that I had described it from a sideways perspective.'
KATHRYN WILLIAMS.

To summarize, foreknowledge also extends to cover unhappy events, some trivial experiences, and a few pleasant pieces of information. As with premonitions of death, foreknowledge of unpleasant events is usually associated with someone known by the percipient, but the victim may sometimes be a total stranger. Foreknowledge of pleasant experiences seems to be closely linked with the percipient's own life. A few variants of foreknowledge exist, apart from ordinary premonitions, including *déjà vu* and premonitory signs or symbols.

# 4

# The Percipients

The overwhelming number of people who report having premonitions are female. In this chapter three typical percipients, all female, will be described, along with their premonitions, to provide a more intimate insight into their life and experiences.

### Barbara Garwell

Barbara Garwell was born 27 July 1929, the seventh child of a seventh child, and her experiences tend to lend weight to the old folk lore that such people are usually sensitive in psychic matters. [1] Over the years Barbara has had many premonitions, mostly in the form of dreams, but also the three other modes of 'reception' (sleep-onset imagery, waking thoughts, and waking imagery). The prior knowledge of events enters Barbara's consciousness spontaneously, with no 'seeking' or training. Her notable cases have concerned violent events, like assassinations and accidents.

Barbara lives in a spick and span bungalow at Aldbrough in North Humberside, and spends her time taking care of her husband Roland and a son. Two older daughters and a son have moved away and married. Her husband was an electrician but he took early retirement after suffering several strokes. Her youngest boy, Jon, has recently left school.

Barbara had a normal childhood which was 'full of happy memories'. She was of average ability at school and left, as many children did in the 1940s, at the age of 14. She became a shop assistant and worked mainly as such in subsequent years. Barbara married at the age of 20, in 1950, and the relationship has been most successful. The Catholic faith is an important part of Barbara's psychology and she attends church regularly.

Her memory is better than average and she also possesses vivid visual imagery; being able to create clear 'pictures in the mind'. As a child she would entertain herself by causing people to appear to shrink or expand in size! Barbara is an energetic person, though she requires little sleep — perhaps only five hours each night. She is 'superstitious' about many things and reports having had a strong phobia of stretches of water since she fell in a lake as a child and was frightened. Another phobia she has is travelling on buses. In personality tests she is found to be somewhat neurotic, tough-minded, conservative, shrewd, affected by feelings, sober, shy, assertive, self-sufficient and rather tense.

Another ability of hers seems to be to foresee the future for individuals using card reading. 'I pick up thoughts when I'm doing it, and they often turn out to be correct' she says. For instance, she detected the imminent death of her mother when reading cards for her sister. Barbara gives an interesting anecdote of apparent telepathy or clairvoyance between herself and Roland. One time when he was away in the forces she felt an incredibly strong urge to go to the railway station to meet him. It seemed quite irrational because he was not due home for weeks, but just as she arrived there with the children, Roland stepped off a train. He had intended to surprise Barbara, but as it happened he was the more amazed! Barbara's life has been full of similar strange 'coincidences'.

### The Sadat assassination
One night in September 1981, Barbara woke from a violent, vivid, coloured dream which she instantly sensed on waking was precognitive. In the dream a sort of stadium was seen, with a single row of seated men all wearing dark pin-striped suits. The men had 'coffee coloured' skin. Barbara 'knew' that sand was nearby and that the setting was somewhere in the Middle East. Two soldiers, also 'coffee coloured', were observed to go up to the row of men and spray then with automatic fire'.[1]

In the morning Barbara discussed the dream with Roland and they attempted to determine which country was to be involved in the coming tragedy. However, they were unable to be specific.

Precisely three weeks later, on Tuesday 6 October 1981, at 12.40 p.m. local time, President Anwar Sadat of Egypt was assassinated, and several other people killed and injured, at the annual military parade commemorating the 1973 Yom Kippur war with Israel. Some soldiers dressed in olive drab uniform ran from a vehicle in the parade to the saluting base where the guests filled several rows of seats. President Sadat was wearing a black uniform. The attackers threw grenades and sprayed the dignitaries with fire from Kalashnikov guns.

This premonition was strikingly accurate. Although the country and the main victim were not identifiable in the dream, the circumstances were so similar that retrospective identificiation is apparent.

The main correct points were:

1. The general setting — a Middle East country.
2. The immediate setting — a stadium, with a row of VIPs.
3. The attackers — 'coffee coloured' soldiers.
4. The type of attack — soldiers running up to the dignitaries in a stadium and firing weapons.
5. The weapons — automatic rifles.

Incorrect points:
1. Several rows of seats were present, not just one.
2. Most of the official guests were in military uniform and were not wearing dark suits, although Sadat did have a black uniform.

Uncertain points:
1. The specific country.
2. The main victim.

Barbara's husband, eldest son, older sister and a brother all confirmed the details of this premonition, stating that it occurred three weeks before the event.

### The assassination attempt on President Reagan
This premonition also came in a dream, in a somewhat symbolic form. It was early March 1981 when Barbara dreamed of being in a large squarish old car 'like an old style Austin'. In the car with her were two Germans in SS uniform. A limousine-type car was

approaching. It stopped and a man got out. He had a 'pockmarked' face and Barbara 'knew' that he was an ex-actor. The two SS men got out of the car and one of them drew a pistol from his leather holster and fired several shots at the actor, who fell. The SS men dashed back to their car and sped off. On waking, Barbara identified the victim, very uncertainly, as Trevor Howard.

On Monday 30 March 1981, three weeks (again) after Barbara's dream, an attempt was made on the life of President Ronald Reagan — a former well-known screen actor. He was getting *into* a car near the Hilton hotel in Washington D.C. Several shots were fired from a pistol by John Warnock Hinckley, the 25-year-old son of a Denver oil tycoon. Reagan was injured, as were his press-secretary, a Secret Service agent and a police officer. The Times newspaper reported two days later that Hinckley had joined the National Socialist party (a neo-Nazi group) in 1978 but was expelled in 1979 because his views were too extreme and violent.

Although the victim in the dream was wrongly identified by Barbara on waking, the links with the Reagan incident are certainly close. It springs to mind at once that the 'Nazi' attacker could have been representative of Hinckley's political persuassion.

The correct points:
1. The immediate setting — a road, near cars, a limousine involved.
2. The attacker — a 'Nazi'.
3. The weapon — a pistol.

Incorrect points:
1. The attacker was with a fellow 'Nazi'. So far as is known, Hinckley operated independently.
2. The attackers were dressed in uniform in the dream.
3. The victim got out of his car in the dream, whereas President Reagan was getting into his vehicle.

The veracity of Barbara's account was again confirmed by several members of her family.

**The *Achille Lauro* fire**
In a vivid dream, also having a special 'precognitive' quality, in November 1981, Barbara observed a ship at sea. Two coffins were

seen to descend slowly over the ship's side, sliding down a sort of rope gangway. Barbara took the ship to be the one on which two friends were shortly to sail; the *Achille Lauro*.

Barbara's friends sometimes travelled to South Africa to visit relatives, either by air or cruise liner. At the time of the dream Barbara was aware that the couple were due to sail in a fortnight. She decided not to tell the couple about the dream in case it caused upset and, anyway, the deaths did not seem to be associated with the couple. The female of the couple had been ill with pneumonia and her husband was in good health.

At 2.40 a.m. on Wednesday 2 December 1981, three weeks (again) after Barbara's dream, a fire broke out in a cocktail bar on the Italian liner *Achille Lauro*, 100 miles off the Canary Islands. The ship, displacing 24,000 tons and captained by Arnaldo Bigiletto, was on the cruise to South Africa. Thick smoke poured through part of the vessel and the resulting disorder two people died of heart attacks. They were Mrs D. Wyborn (aged 51) and Mr Summers (aged 71). Mr Summer's wife apparently jumped or fell overboard and was lost. The fire was brought under control and the ship put into Las Palmas for repairs to the electrical system. Barbara's friends were unharmed, although shaken.

Correct items:
1. The general environment — at sea.
2. The immediate setting — a large liner.
3. The number of bodies taken off the ship (two). A third body was not recovered.

Incorrect point:
1. No fire was seen in the dream.

Statements were obtained from two sisters and a friend to back up this premonition.

The three dreams investigated here came from one year, so the number of precognitions experienced by Barbara during her life so far may have been considerable. One purpose of examining a number of observations is to search for possible consistencies which might lead to a better understanding of the phenomenon. Supposing that these cases were indeed true precognitions, and taking the two assassination dreams, it is noted that in both:

1.   The environment was predicted accurately.
2.   The attackers were described accurately in an important respect (soldiers; 'Nazi').
3.   The weapons were described accurately.
4.   The victim, although not clearly identifiable in the dream could be ascertained by an intelligent guess.

Another noticeable factor was that the time period between premonition and fulfilment was the same in all three cases, which in itself enhances the acceptability of a psi explanation. If the points listed are repeatable elements, hopefully future examples can be 'interpreted' more exactly, perhaps resulting in the avoidance of catastrophes.

Conceivably, the non-specificity concerning the victim might arise from a lack of information on that point 'at source', or a limitation of the dreaming process which can only refer to the victim indirectly by association.

### The analysis of collected premonitions
Barbara readily agreed to participate in a unique and important experiment concerning premonitions. A major criticism has always applied to studies of premonitions. It is that the material might have been selected by the percipient from a larger body of cases that did not achieve fulfilment. The purpose of the experiment would be to overcome that objection by getting Barbara to send me an account of each premonition, immediately it was 'received'. Only that data would be analysed, and the duration would be one year (the whole of 1982).[2]

At the end of the year, 52 premonitions had been sent in the pre-paid envelopes. Two 'blind judges' who knew nothing about the experiments were given half the reports each (Judge One: quarters one and three; Judge two: quarters two and four) and asked to search through the local paper (which contains both local and international news) for the 28 days ahead of the date of each premonition. If a story was seen that seemed to be related to the premonition either directly or symbolically, it was given a rating-score (0 = none; 1–2 = slight; 3–4 = fair; 5–6 = good; 7–8 = very good). The 28 day period was used because Barbara reported that most of her premonitions came to fruition within that time.

The judging was conducted in 1985. In fact, the judges rated each premonition against newspaper items from each of *two* years, firstly the 'real' year, and secondly a 'control' year. The judges believed that the premonitions were a random mixture from both years.

Obviously, if the premonitions were relating to newspaper items for the month ahead, the ratings should be higher each time for the actual year rather than the control year. A statistical test could determine whether this was so or not.

The data was deliberately analysed over-cautiously, and the result approached statistical significance. The standard mode of testing would have produced a result that was certainly statistically significant. 19 of the 52 premonitions showed a higher rank in the true year over the control year, while eight showed the reverse. The other cases showed no rank, or tied.

So it seems that some effect was operating, according to the statistical analysis. However, additional evidence was supplied by the finding that previously noted consistent latency effects (the time from premonition to fulfilment) appeared also in this data. The three week latency has already been mentioned concerning the dreams. A three-day latency was seen and published in a report concerning visual-imagery premonitions collected in 1981. The three highest scoring premonitions in the experiment all corresponded with events in the true year, and each fitted the previously noted latency period:

1. Rating: 8.

Barbara had always posted any premonitions to me, but on Monday 10 May 1982, she telephoned me saying that she had experienced a very strong premonition concerning the Pope. It was a visual-image type. Barbara sent me the following written account:

> 'As I got into bed I closed my eyes and saw the outside of a castle. From the castle came about eight choir-boys or altar-boys. There were a lot of people together and much confusion. In the centre of these people I saw a figure in white. It was a person of state; e.g. the Pope.'

Three days later, at the Fatima shrine in Portugal, a man attempted to stab the Pope with a bayonet.

## 2. Rating: 7.

'I had a vivid dream. Ron (Roland) was sat at an old table reading a newspaper as if he had just picked it up. The headline was "Boat broke in two — sinking". There was a picture. It was coming to England. *HMS Diddy*? I felt that it was an old one, an oil tanker, as there were no portholes. It was sinking in the water. It seemed to be a Greek ship. Ron's mother said, "All the people said to me the water was boiling".'

On Saturday 13 February 1982, on the front page of the *Hull Daily Mail* appeared a story about a Greek vessel, *Victory*, which was sinking in the Atlantic. It was a tanker and was sailing to Liverpool from Florida. In a severe gale the ship split in two. I was in a newspaper office at the time and saw the agency tapes. The sea was described by the crew as 'boiling'. Incidentally, 'Diddy' is a word specifically linked with the city of Liverpool.

## 3. Rating: 6.

'I got into bed and shut my eyes. I immediately got a clear picture, as if on a cinema screen. It was an island with whitish buildings. It seemed to move as if projected to me (the length of the island). It was not a big island. There was a huge stretch of what seemed to be bluish water in front of it. Then I saw lots and lots of boats. It seemed to me as if they were facing each other for attack. They were definitely boats, not ships. Across the front of this screen was a whole length of foreign words that I could not understand. It was so real; like watching a TV screen. This was the clearest visual experience I have ever had.'

The Argentinian invasion of the Falkland Islands occurred suddenly and unexpectedly on 2 April 1982, three days after this premonition. Throughout the period of hostilities British TV sometimes showed Argentinian film of the war, and this was often accompanied by Spanish text on the screen, similar to Barbara's account.

There were several near-misses in the premonitions which were not rated because they fell outside the specified 28 day period. In one premonition Barbara was anxious for a large group of children in a vehicle of transportation. Seven weeks later a coach crash happened in France, killing 48 children. Another premonition told of the death of Mrs Gandhi. That event did not take place until two years later.

Since this experiment there have been numerous other cases of Barbara having foreseen events. Just one further example among many is the following:

In December 1984 Barbara met a healer called Leonard. He visited Barbara's home to impart healing to Roland and Barbara. On the second visit, while Barbara's back was being treated, she closed her eyes and saw clear imagery of traffic lights. She immediately felt concerned for Leonard and told him to be careful while crossing the road at traffic lights. She reminded him again as he was leaving. Five days later Leonard was struck by a motor cycle while crossing a road at traffic lights and died shortly afterwards. More recently, she foresaw the 1987 Stock Market collapse, and the terrible disaster in the Philippines in December 1987, when 2000 people died as a ferry sank.

Barbara, then, continues to experience premonitions. They are by no means all correct, but a number are uncannily close to later incidents. The consistent latency effects are intriguing. The longer period for dream-based premonitions could be a sign that the REM state is more sensitive to precognitive material than the waking state at sleep-onset and has a longer 'range' into the future.

## Sandra MacDonald

Sandra MacDonald is an ordinary housewife who lives in Grimsby. She was born on 26 April 1954 and describes her childhood as having been normal. She has a younger brother. Sandra says she got on well with her father and reasonably so with her mother. At the age of 15 Sandra left school, not having gained any academic qualifications. She got a job as a sales assistant selling handbags. Sandra married a fisherman in 1978 and had a daughter, but she separated from her husband in 1981.

According to personality tests some of her major traits are: assertiveness, forthrightness, tenseness. She also scores high on neuroticism.

### The Artemis premonition

On the night of Wednesday 23 June 1971 Sandra, then 17, had a very vivid dream in which she saw the submarine *HMS Artemis* sink.[3] A wall was apparent near the vessel, so she presumed that the incident happened in a harbour. There was a 'scramble' of men on board and she 'knew' that three men were trapped inside the submarine. She also had the impression that she knew two of the trapped men, and that two of the three died. The submarine was seen to sink slowly and completely. Sandra related the dream next day to her mother and to several friends over the next few days.

Now the background to the experience is important. A week before the dream the *Artemis* had made a visit to Grimsby and Sandra had met several of the crew, for the first time, at a dance. She became particularly friendly with one of them and had also been shown over the submarine.

At 7.15 p.m. on Thursday 1 July 1971, the 'A' class submarine *HMS Artemis* sank at her moorings at Gosport, Hampshire. The vessel, 282 feet long and displacing 1500 tons, sank stern first and disappeared into 40 feet of water in a minute or two.

Ten crewmen had been on watch and there were three visiting sea cadets on board. The Chief Petty Officer, David Guest, ran through the vessel making sure that people were escaping to the deck, but he and two other submariners had to lock themselves into a watertight torpedo storage section, and so became trapped. Those who got away jumped overboard. Incredibly, it was not possible to shut most of the watertight bulkhead doors because a temporary power cable ran throughout the length of the submarine. The three trapped men remained incarcerated for 10½ hours before emerging from an underwater escape hatch. The submarine was raised to the surface on 6 July.

What had happened was that a ballast tank had been flooded previously to improve the submarine's stability on being towed from Portsmouth, but the procedure left two hatches very close to the water line. At the time of the incident the fuel tanks were being filled with water, a process known as 'first filling'. Eventually, because the submarine was so low in the water, the hatches dipped beneath the surface and water flowed into the vessel.

Three people who Sandra stated had been told of her dream before the sinking were contacted in order to check her story. They were an ex-member of the crew who at the time of the sinking was an Ordnance Electrical Mechanic (1st Class); a female friend of the percipient; and Sandra's mother. All three witnesses confirmed in writing that Sandra's account was correct. I also inspected Sandra's diary and saw her notes of the dream and the sinking.

The possibility that something in the percipient's history somehow 'sensitizes' that person to a particular type of precogniton is raised by the fact that Sandra's father escaped from a trawler which sank in the North Sea.

Also, it should be noted that another newspaper item on 1 July 1971 was of the death of three soviet cosmonauts. They perished when their re-entry vehicle depressurized catastrophically. These men could also be said to have been 'trapped inside the vessel'. Was there a link between the premonition and the Soyuz disaster? Was the *Artemis* premonition somehow reinforced by the conceptually-similar Soyuz event? Or was the premonition really about Soyuz, but portrayed in imagery familiar to the percipient?

Sandra reports a number of other premonitions, including the following:

'I dreamed that my brother had an accident in a red car. He didn't have a car at the time. He went to Newcastle some times later to pick one up, a red car, and he crashed it.'

'I dreamed that my boss, Mrs Arnold, had fallen down stairs. A few weeks later, she came in and said she had fallen down some stairs in a London Department store.'

'I had a nightmare. There was a door and behind it I "knew" there was a coffin. I was terrified and sensed death and decay. There was a car outside. Someone was running to the car. I thought "Don't get in the car". Shortly afterwards I heard that someone I knew was killed in a car crash. I had a similar dream of a coffin about my grandfather. It happened about six months later.'

'I was going abroad with a friend. I had a dream that an airport coach had a yellow and black streak, and that something would go wrong. We went to London and found that the coach to Luton was just like the one in my dream. Also, the plane had the same streak. I was frightened and did not want to fly. The plane taxied out but returned. It had engine trouble. We flew out later in the same plane.'

Sandra is perhaps typical of percipients who have occasional premonitions; some of which are quite striking and certainly bear rigorous investigation. Over the years the volume of cases becomes impressive. It is this unremitting frequency that is highly convincing of a paranormal effect operating.

### Lesley Brennan

Lesley Brennan is an attractive, intelligent woman with a soft, well-mannered voice. She is broad-minded and witty and has a superficially 'bubbly' personality, although various worries and monthly physiological changes can make her depressed sometimes. She is a housewife and was born on 16 February 1950.

Lesley's premonitions have been few, but one in particular provides a truly outstanding case of a waking hallucination of a totally unexpected future calamity, the Flixborough chemical plant explosion. The premonition came out of the blue. Lesley had never paid much attention to telepathy, clairvoyance or precognition, so her special sensitivity was in no way practised or polished. On the other hand it is possible that several other premonitions of a similar type may have gone unnoticed to her.

Her childhood was reportedly stressful. It seems that a rather dominating and aggressive father may have been cruel to her mother and three brothers, although Lesley was not the victim so much herself. Two of her three brothers are twins. Two, including one twin, suffer from epilepsy, which is controlled by medication.

At school Lesley excelled and at Grammar school she acquired seven 'O' level passes. Her favourite subject was music, and she played the viola, reaching Grade five in examinations. She plays in the Grimsby Symphony Orchestra.

Lesley married in 1968 and had two children, but she divorced her husband and was waiting for the Decree Absolute at the time of her major premonition. Her job then was cashier at the local bank. Lesley remarried in 1978 and had another child, but that marriage foundered too. In 1987 Lesley married for the third time.

Personality measurements represent Lesley as being venturesome, intelligent, self-assured and affected by feelings. After the birth of her third child, Lesley says she developed a strong phobia of knives for some reason. However, she overcame the fear out of necessity when she started a part-time job at a factory where she had to use a knife in her work.

### The Flixborough disaster

At about noon on Saturday 1 June 1974, Lesley, who was then living in Cleethorpes, was watching TV alone. The word 'newsflash' appeared on the screen and a male voice gave news of an explosion at Flixborough, some 40 km away. Several people had been killed and injured, the voice said. Lesley felt shocked and shortly afterwards she told a couple who were staying in the same house who came in for lunch. That evening they saw television reports of the disaster but could not understand why the time of the explosion was given as late afternoon. The next day, on reading that the explosion had indeed happened, Lesley and her friends realized that she had experienced a premonition. [4]

At 4:53 p.m. on Saturday 1 June 1974 at the Nypro (UK) Ltd chemical plant at Flixborough, South Humberside, a massive explosion occurred which virtually demolished the 60 acre complex. The disaster happened suddenly and unexpectedly, resulting in 28 deaths and hundreds of injuries. The effects of the blast were widespread: 1,821 houses and 167 shops and factories in the vicinity reported damage.

The plant had been producing, annually, some 70,000 tons of caprolactam, which is a basic raw material for Nylon 6. The Official Report of the catastrophe found that a 20 inch temporary bypass pipe had ruptured, releasing a large vapour cloud of cyclohexane at 155°C, which ignited producing an explosion 'of warlike dimensions' equivalent to some 15–45 tons of T.N.T.

The two witnesses were questioned closely. One was a male welder with a local engineering firm, and the female worked in the same bank as Lesley. Both witnesses signed statements confirming that Lesley reported the explosion to them at lunchtime, 1 June 1974.

BBC and ITV stations were questioned about a newsflash of any description that went out that lunchtime. No newsflash on any topic was transmitted that lunchtime. Since no actual item was transmitted, how was it that Lesley saw one? Either she hallucinated the newsflash, perhaps in a brief sleep (and included a possibly sub-consciously perceived piece of premonitory information) or, by some unknown means, her TV alone received a modified signal. The former surely seems most likely, but since no one else was present in the room, the point is not actually certain.

It is significant to consider that Flixborough did not figure at all in Lesley's psychology. She knew no one who worked at the plant and the location simply did not enter into her mind normally.

Was it possible that Lesley's experience was not a premonition, but that she picked up telepathically a worry in the mind of an engineer at the plant? That seems not to be so, because when the shift changed at 3 p.m. (after her premonition), it was simply reported that a reactor was slightly faulty. But it was not thought to be serious. Also, had Lesley somehow picked up a clairvoyant picture of a reactor fault it is doubtful whether it would have been meaningful to Lesley.

One factor that may have been conducive to the premonition was that Lesley's life was rather stressful at the time. She herself feels that her premonitions occur in association with some unhappiness about something.

Actually, a second premonition, also of an explosion, was experienced by Lesley in 1980. However, it was not witnessed. Lesley says that while taking her baby round to a friend's house on the morning of 24 June at about 9 a.m., she felt compelled to take a different route from usual. Going along Welholme Road, Grimsby, a strange thought entered her head. It was 'wouldn't it be awful if a gas explosion happened in one of these houses, while children are nearby.' She did not tell anyone of her notion 'in case it sounded odd'. At lunchtime (12.30) that same day, an accidental gas cylinder explosion occurred at 153 Welholme Road. The premises were severely damaged but no one was hurt.

Lesley may have a special sensitivity for detecting explosions a few hours ahead and might conceivably be useful in providing fore-warning of accidents or natural (and even nuclear) catastrophes.

In 1982, Lesley reported another incident. She went to her temporary job and immediately felt 'faint all over'. She had a strong thought; 'wouldn't it be terrible if I slipped and knocked my head against something'. There were heavy steel trays around. A few hours later a woman working at the same place on the next shift had such an accident, requiring five stiches.

Lesley's experience concerning Flixborough is extraordinarily compelling as an example of premonition. Although the nature of it may seem peculiar (in the form of a TV newsflash), it constitutes a certain recognized sub-group which will be described in the next chapter.

The case was not discovered after diligent searching. After having had my own apparent premonition on the Humber ferry (described in Chapter 1), as soon as I met my psychologist friend in Grimsby I asked him if he knew anyone who had experienced a premonition. He then informed me of Lesley's premonition of the

Flixborough disaster. Lesley is my friend's niece.

The evidence for foreknowledge that has been given so far in this book is based on personal accounts. Its strength is that it is about *real* premonitions occurring in natural circumstances. Scientifically, though, it does not reach exact standards because the cases did not take place under scientific scrutiny. The next step in this exploration of the area is to look at what has been found in scientific studies of foreknowledge.

# 5

# Science and Foreknowledge

There are two broad scientific approaches to trying to understand foreknowledge. The first involves establishing an artificial laboratory set-up to test simple precognition, where all the elements can be controlled experimentally in order to see precisely how the phenomenon operates. This technique of 'manipulating the variables' is used by psychologists routinely. Unfortunately, in the unique case of precognition, which seems to be closely associated with personal/emotional features, there is a potential problem that in trying to reduce the phenomenon to its component parts in the cold impersonal laboratory, any real effect might be dissected out of existence. Nevertheless, some interesting results have emerged from studies.

The other avenue of exploration is to look at 'real' examples of premonition, either in large numbers; superficially, so as to obtain average characteristics; or by investigating and confirming individual cases. This approach is valuable because it throws light on actual cases of premonition in the natural environment in which they occur.

A point to mention here with regard to laboratory studies of precognition is that it is difficult to be sure that precognition alone was responsible for any positive results. If, say, a subject is guessing which number on a die is to appear at the next throw, it could be that the subject uses mind-over-matter (PK) to cause the die to fall in a certain way. Some studies are designed so that the likelihood of the inclusion of PK is exceedingly remote, for instance, where the selection of a 'target' to be guessed is determined by air-temperature readings somewhere.

Another possibility is that the subject might possibly in some circumstances pick up information telepathically from someone who knows what is to happen. There is yet another possibility that the subject observes clairvoyantly something that could indicate what will happen. These are theoretical considerations which have to be taken into account when planning precognition experiments.

## Drawing experiments

British psychologist W. Whately-Carington performed a set of pioneering experiments in telepathy at Cambridge in the 1930s.[1] His method was to select a drawable word from a dictionary using random-number tables each day. A picture of the object was then drawn and hung up in his home from 7 p.m. to 9.30 a.m. Hundreds of people in several countries tried to guess the word using any telepathic abilities they might have. The data was rated by a 'naive' judge, that is, one who did not know about the purpose of the experiment and so could not bias the results consciously or unconsciously.

Carington found that there was statistically strong evidence for telepathy, but further analysis revealed significant post and pre-cognitive effects i.e. people often tended to be correct about those pictures displayed a night or two before or after the one for which they were aiming. Carington mentioned this 'displacement' effect to the mathematician and experimenter in parapsychology, S.G. Soal.[2] Soal re-examined data from some non-significant telepathic experiments with Gloria Stewart and Basil Shackleton and said that he found a similar displacement phenomenon. Soal went on to conduct many well-known experiments. However all his work must now be considered to be highly suspect because a brilliant piece of computerized detection work by statistician Betty Marwick in 1978 showed that he had been dishonest with at least some of his data. Unfortunately, fraud does turn up sometimes, in *all* branches of science.[3]

## Card-guessing

J.B. Rhine firmly established laboratory testing of psi phenomena in the US at Duke University in the 1930s.[4]. Telepathy, clairvoyance and precognition were studied in the simplest form using 'neutral' symbols on cards (Zener cards). The symbols were a square, circle, star, cross, and wavy-lines. Subjects spent hours guessing which card was the chosen 'target' over thousands of trials. Psychokinesis was also investigated thoroughly by Rhine and his workers.

The results offered by Rhine gave clear statistical evidence of these phenomena, and yet the sheer unreasoned antagoism of many 'scientists' to the area ensured tht parapsychology could not be elevated to a 'respectable' academic subject.

## Random-number generator studies

A very successful series of psi experiments, which dealt with precognition, has been produced by Dr Helmut Schmidt in the US. He introduced the random-number generator (based on the decay of a radio-active source) with a fully automated method for recording subjects' guesses. The RNG caused one of a panel of lights to be switched on immediately after the subect had guessed which it was it was to be and the guess had been registered.

Schmidt has had to select high scoring subjects from larger groups, but his findings with those gifted subjects have been statistically phenomenal. In one experiment, taking over 63,000 trials, or guesses, three subjects produced results which were over 500 million to one against such a chance result!

In a number of well thought out experiments Schmidt has attempted to sort out whether precognition, PK, or clairvoyance has been operating in previous findings. He attempted to exclude PK in one study by using paper-tape storing random numbers. The moving tape stopped immediately after the subject had recorded the guess. At that moment the 'target' was selected. The results were significant and showed that precognition, or clairvoyance, could have been responsible. In other work he showed that mind power (PK) can be used to affect a random number generator.

The only alternative to the psi hypothesis in these experiments is that Schmidt deliberately cheated, but there is no evidence to support that idea. Some of his findings have been confirmed by laboratories in different parts of the world, but non-significant results have also appeared with some researchers. Since gifted subjects would seem to be a crucial factor in these experiments, studies giving negative results might have used unsuitable subjects.

Or, odd as it may seem, perhaps the experimenter's own attitude to the outcome may actually determine the result.

Schmidt's discoveries are greatly anomalous to those viewing the topic from an ordinary traditional scientific position. They suggest that a radical shift in our perspective of all things is necessary in order to comprehend the true state of affairs in the universe.

## Dream precognition

The dream state is very often responsible for psi information, and it is not surprising that experiments have been conducted in the sleep-laboratory situation into telepathy and precognition. Nearly all these studies have sought simultaneous telepathy between a sleeping, dreaming 'receiver' person and an awake 'transmitter' person, but two very interesting investigations into precognition were carried out in America using a British 'sensitive', Malcolm Bessent.

They were part of a long series of dreams and psi experiments performed by a team headed by Montague Ullman and Stanley Krippner, from the Maimonides hospital in New York.[5] The technique used in the Bessent studies was to obtain dream reports over several nights from him. In the morning, an 'experience' was randomly selected for Bessent to go through. For instance, in one trial the word 'corridor' was randomly chosen and an art print titled *Corridor of the St Paul Hospital*, by Van Gogh, was obtained. Malcolm had to play the role of a mental patient walking through a corridor at a mental asylum. Malcolm had dreamed a few hours previously of a 'large concrete building' from which a patient was trying to escape. Independent judges rated how close the set-up experiences were to the subject's dreams for that previous night.

The odds were very highly significant in favour of the precognitive hypothesis. If the result had been a fluke then it would have occurred only once in several thousand similar experiments. Even more impressive, a follow-up experiment again produced a highly significant result. These experiments supplied the best scientific evidence yet for precognition occurring in the dream state.

## The 'dream machine' and precognition

In the course of the author's extensive research into 'lucid' dreams (conscious, controllable dreaming), a device called the 'dream machine' was invented and patented.[6] It is a small, portable electronic bedside unit which has various functions including (a) increasing dream recall; (b) preventing nightmares; (c) experimentally inducing 'lucid' dreaming. Anyone is capable of using the device at home.

It operates by monitoring the user's breathing rate, which often increases during periods of dreaming (REM sleep). The user presets a respiratory rate suitable for him/her which, when reached, will 'trigger' the device, so sounding an audible alarm to gently waken the dreamer after a variable delay.[7] Alternatively, the unit may automatically administer tactile pulses to the dreamer, so causing 'lucidity' within the dream with some users. The device can increase dream recall greatly — material that would not normally be available to memory. In fact, we dream for some two hours each night, but our typical recall is exceedingly fragmentary.

There is the possibility that hidden in all that forgotten dream material is much precognitive information, so the dream machine may prove to be a useful investigative tool in future studies.[8] The reason for that opinion is reinforced by the fact that one woman, Pamela Green, reported being woken from the following dream:

> 'I was in a high building. There was a large plate glass window, and a balustrade with a wooden top. There were pink and grey zigzag curtains.
>
> 'I looked out of the window down a hill. There were buildings, and roads with traffic. At the bottom of the hill I saw a building which I "knew" was a cinema. It had lights on it but I could not make out the name. The building I was in had two entrances at the front (on left and right corners) and I "knew" that parking was not possible in the front and that I had come from a car park at the side and had to walk the whole length of the front of the building to an entrance that was open.'

The device's alarm woke Pamela at that point and she noted down the dream. Two days later Pamela visited Bradford. It was a place she had been to before when she was 12. On arrival Pamela went to the Information section of a library and obtained a list of local museums and places of interest. She decided to visit the National Museum of Photography. Parking was not possible in front of the building, so a walk was necessary from the side to the far front corner entrance. The other entrance, on the far left corner, was closed.

Pamela went to the 5th floor of the modern building and reports being utterly amazed at seeing the details of her dream, although the curtains were not there. On looking out of the window she observed the scene just as in her dream, and where the cinema was in the dream she saw a cinema with lights spelling out the word 'Odeon'. The sense of recognition was considerable and Pamela telephoned me excitedly about the strange episode.

Now an explanation solely in terms of precognition is not strictly permissible here because, for instance, Pamela may have seen a panoramic photo of the scene which she unconsciously revived in the dream. But the dream could conceivably have contained psi information, so there is potential for people to perform their own studies into precognition in their dreams.

Pamela was woken at a moment of physiological arousal, with an elevated breathing rate, but not that of a nightmare. This state of moderate arousal may reflect the typical bodily condition associated with psi in dreams, in which case the device could be ideal for identifying those moments.

### Animal studies

A landmark experiment, seeking precognition in animals, was performed by two French zoologists in the 1960s. To protect their names in the French academic Establishment, they had to go to the preposterous length of publishing under the pseudonyms of Duval and Montredom.[9] Actually, it has been learned since that the senior author was the eminent Professor Remy Chauvin of the Sorbonne University.

In the automated experiment mice were placed in a box which had a central barrier. The floor on either side of the barrier could be electrified alternately via a random number generator. The mice were found to have avoided approaching shocks by jumping the barrier, at a highly significant level statistically i.e. precognition was a possible explanation.

In the US, a series of similar experiments were published over the next few years. However another very unwelcome case of experimenter fraud was exposed in that work. W.J. Levy was caught cheating by his students and resigned his post.[10] He had produced many results in support of animal psi, but all his data must now be totally disregarded. The sceptics took full advantage of the situation, as can be imagined.

Since then, the French workers repeated their experiment twice and on both occasions got positive results. In addition, several other researchers in different countries have shown apparent psi effects in various animal species, although a few studies have not been successful.

Let us pause for a moment here to think about the implications of psi in animals. It seems reasonable that if psi exists it should have developed as part of the evolutionary process to aid survival. But it also seems likely that psi counter-measures would also have been refined. Perhaps, then, the more advanced species have *less* overall psi because the abilities have been neutralized. Simple animals might well be the best subjects in psi experiments. If a certain degree of brain organization is required for psi, it should be possible to determine that level and draw relevant conclusions about the nature of psi. Clearly, a very important way to study psi is to look at species' similarities and differences.

Turning now from laboratory studies, which may be criticized for not dealing with precognition in real-life situations, what detailed investigations have been made of spontaneous premonitions happening to people?

### L.E. Rhine's analysis[11]

Louisa Rhine, wife of the great parapsychologist J.B. Rhine, conducted a thorough analysis of a large number of cases of precognition in comparison with a large number of simultaneous (telepathy) cases. The purpose was to observe any noticeable differences between the two types of experience on three features:

1.  The state of consciousness of the individual (asleep or awake),
2.  The type of premonition. Rhine categorized the forms as: Intuition — a waking idea; Hallucinatory — a sensory impression; Unrealistic dreaming — a day dream; Realistic dreaming — usually a dream,
3.  The degree of conviction* or certainty accompanying the experience.

Firstly, she looked at 1,324 precognitive cases, and 1,966

simultaneous ones. The proportion of dreams to waking experiences was considerably more in the precognitive cases (68%) than in the simultaneous cases (35%). As to the type of experience, there were also differences:

|                      | Precognitive | Simultaneous |
| -------------------- | ------------ | ------------ |
| Intuition            | 19%          | 35%          |
| Hallucinatory        | 6%           | 25%          |
| Unrealistic dreaming | 15%          | 21%          |
| Realistic dreaming   | 60%          | 19%          |

In the precognitive group, 36 per cent carried conviction, while in the simultaneous group, the figure was 62 per cent. When just dreams were compared, since most precognitive experiences are dreams, 19 per cent of the precognitive cases carried conviction while 40 per cent of the telepathy cases carried conviction.

The data from which Rhine calculated the results in fact consisted of two separate sets. She then separated the data to see if the results applied to both, and did indeed find that the differences were consistent in both collections.

However, perhaps Rhine's findings are not so unexpected because, after all, simultaneous experiences are most likely to happen during the day when both victim and percipient are awake. The amount of conviction, too, might naturally be expected to be more in simultaneous cases, if only because there is a greater probability, known to the percipient, that the event could be happening at that moment.

## L.E. Rhine's study of intervention [12]

In this work, Rhine dealt with the question of whether an event that has been forewarned can be avoided, i.e. whether 'intervention' is feasible. She looked for cases among reports that had previously been classified into those where the percipient was convinced that something would happen. There were 574 such accounts, but those where the precognized event was favourable (e.g. a lottery win) were discarded, so leaving 433 to be examined.

The cases were divided according to whether intervention had been attempted or not. Another selection separated out those that could have been prevented as against those that could not. They were then analysed according to whether the intervention failed or succeeded.

Rhine observed that in nearly two-thirds of the cases no intervention was attempted, so her study was aimed at 191 cases where intervention was tried. In 60 of these the attempt failed for a number of reasons. The information may have been inadequate, or the victim may have been unco-operative. In 131 cases an intervention was tried and was successful. One example was the following:

'On 9 February 1942, Mr and Mrs C stopped for the night at a small hotel in Selma, N.C. Early the next morning Mrs C dreamed that the hotel was reduced to burning ruins by an explosion. The dream woke her and she was unable to go back to sleep. Waking her husband she insisted that they leave at once. Mr C. heavy with sleep, protested loudly that they had not planned to leave for hours. But his wife was determined and they departed at once.

'A day later Mrs C called her husband's attention to a story in the morning paper. It was an account of how a truck loaded with dynamite had crashed into a small hotel and the result of the explosion had destroyed the building. The hotel was the one in which they had stayed the night before. If they had stuck to their original schedule they would still have been in the hotel when the truck load of death arrived.'[13]

However, Rhine stated that in 122 of the 131 reports, pure precognition might not have been operating. Telepathy or clairvoyance might have been functioning instead. There were only a few acceptable cases, such as this one:

'When about 19 years old, I got a job that I had been after for a year. The night before I was to report for work as a fireman in a steam plant, I dreamed the same dream three times of a steam explosion in which I was blown out of the building and died in the hospital. I thought that I read the account in the paper. I did not take the job.

About a week later the accident occurred. The man who took my job was blown out of the building and died. One was scalded to death, and one was lost for some time by being blown under a huge pile of coal. I do not know how the fourth man escaped. I helped repair the firebox on the Sterling boiler that let go.'[14]

Rhine offered just nine accounts as being not *proof* of intervention, but as good illustrations to suggest that it might happen.

## An accident survey

The American parapsychologist W.E. Cox carried out a most useful survey in 1956 which leads us to believe that premonitions can affect peoples' behaviour so as to avoid disasters in some cases. [15] Ingeniously, he looked at passenger statistics for the train system in the U.S. He discovered that significantly fewer people travelled in the trains that were involved in accidents than in those same trains on other comparable 'control' days.

What we do not know is how many of those people who avoided the accidents acted on conscious premonitions, and how many had some form of unconscious warning. What kind of excuses did people have for not travelling in the doomed train? Maybe they did actually sense trouble, but perhaps some developed psychosomatic illnesses while others suddenly thought of something more 'important' to do elsewhere. Much further research in this area is an obvious necessity.

There might be characteristic unconscious premonitory avoidance behaviours which, if we could learn what they are, would be of great practical value in our avoiding other disasters in future. If, say, the number of passengers on a ship was unusually low, and the cancellations followed a consistent pre-disaster pattern then the calamity might possibly be averted for the remaining passengers. Consider too the behaviour of astronauts before the launch of a space vehicle. An accident might be detectable in the crew's behaviour in the days before the flight, perhaps manifested by a slight symptom (such as an itchy skin) or excessive interest in some distraction. Detailed behaviour profiling might become part of every astronaut's life.

### The Aberfan study

On 21 October 1966, at 9.15 a.m. after a period of heavy rain, a huge coal tip shifted and engulfed a school at Aberfan in Wales. 144 people were killed, including 128 children. Consultant psychiatrist John Barker visited the site the next day and was greatly affected by the tragedy. [16] He wondered whether there had been any premonitions of the event which could have averted the disaster.

In conjunction with journalist Peter Fairley, an appeal was made in the press for any accounts of foreknowledge concerning the incident. Barker received a total of 76 replies, mostly from the London area. Sixty of them were investigated further. After writing and requesting names and addresses of witnesses, Barker was eventually left with 24 cases. In 36 of the total letters, the premonition was in the form of a dream. The remainder were visions or feelings of unease. In a few cases, the event was sensed at 'home circles'.

Remarkably, one of the premonitions had actually been reported by a victim of the slide. A 10 year old girl, Eryl Jones, told her mother on the very morning of the disaster of a dream she had. Her mother said she didn't have time to listen, but the child insisted. She dreamed that 'something black had come down over the school'. It was a strangely accurate dream and may well have been premonitory. The only devaluing factor is that the huge coal tip, which towered menacingly above the village, may have appeared quite frequently in the villagers' dreams.

A woman from Plymouth informed Barker that she had 'seen' the disaster the night before it happened, and had told her neighbour a few hours before the news came through. At a 'private circle meeting', the woman had imagery of an old school house in a valley. She then saw a Welsh miner and an avalanche of coal, and underneath was a little boy with a long fringe. She then saw rescue operations. While watching a TV programme about the disaster subsequently, she says she saw the same boy and a rescuer from her 'vision'.

In three cases the name Aberfan, or similar, featured in the premonition and the actual date was given by two subjects.

Barker's subjects ranged from 10 to 73 years of age. Women outnumbered men by about five to one. Many of the correspondents stated that they had experienced premonitions before. The vast majority had no links with Aberfan at all. Barker met five of the percipients personally and was impressed by their sincerity.

Interestingly, Barker noticed symptoms of an acute anxiety state in the reported behaviour of several percipients. He conjectured that some individuals may, effectively, be 'human seismographs', able to detect major calamities. He describe a 'pre-disaster syndrome' that affected many of the subjects both psychologically and physically. Symptoms included depression, anxiety, apprehension, unease, loss of concentration, and a sense of suffocation in some people.

Barker recognized the main unsatisfactory aspect of the investigation; that the information was collected *after* the event. Unfortunately, there was no baseline data with which to compare his findings. On any one night in England many people would dream of mine disasters and the like.

Nevertheless, Barker thought it would be interesting to see whether the symptoms of anxiety in some of the subjects might be manifested before other disasters, so providing a 'reliable index of impending calamities'.

Barker promulgated the idea of a computerized 'Premonitions Bureau', where percipients could deposit premonitions. The purpose would be to issue early warning of disasters. It might operate not so much by specific individual premonitions but by looking at 'peaks' and 'patterns' in the incoming information.

## A survey by Hearne

A footnote to a newspaper article about the author's research into premonitions appealed to readers to write in with their own accounts. Some 450 letters were received in total. The overwhelming majority reported having had more than one premonition. The most impressive multiple report cases, totalling 127, were chosen for further study. Those subjects were sent a questionnaire concerning their premonitions, and a personality test. [17]

Of the 127 persons who were sent the questionnaire, 88 responded, which is quite a good return for such studies. About 9 out of 10 of the subjects were female. Their ages ranged from 23 to 80, and the average was 46 years. Looking at subjects' ages in 10 year blocks, most subjects were in their thirties. Half the subjects were in employment, the others consisted of housewives, unemployed and retired people. Almost three-quarters of the sample were married, a fifth were separated, divorced or widowed, and the rest were single.

One question sought to find who else in the subject's family experienced premonitions. So far as was known. Of the 88 subjects, 47 reported positively. The numbers of close relatives having premonitions are shown in Figure 1.

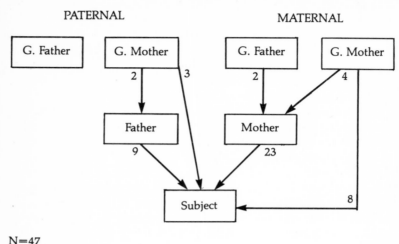

N=47

Figure 1   *Future-seers in the family, as reported by percipients.*

Overall, the ability does seem to be particularly concentrated on the female side of the genetic line, but it must be noted that almost half the subjects reported no family links. How much is genetic and how much due to conditioning is hard to separate.

Regarding the number of premonitions reported by these subjects, four out of 10 stated that the number was between two and 10 premonitions in all, about a third said between 10 and 50, and a fifth estimated that the total exceeded 50! Clearly, premonitions are not isolated phenomena occurring randomly in the population. They seem to concentrate in certain people.

The age at which the first premonition was noticed by the subjects varied from three to 64 years, with an arithmetic average of 18 years. However, most percipients had their first premonition between 10 and 15 years of age.

Subjects were asked to estimate the frequency of their premonitions. In about four out of 10 persons they happened once a year or longer. A further four out of 10 thought it was a matter of months between premonitions on average. One in 10 said it was one or more a week. A further one in 10 stated that the frequency varied greatly so a precise frequency was not possible to determine.

A little over half the sample considered that their premonitions tended to occur in 'batches'.

As to the medical background of the respondents, about four out of 10 reported that they had suffered some form of serious illness at one time or another, and a third said they were currently taking medication. It was noticed that several premonitions occurred to women in advanced pregnancy.

In reponse to a question about any link between stress and premonitions, about six out of 10 stated that their life was not stressful at those times. About three out of 10 said it was stressful, and the others did not know. Nearly all the participants could NOT see any links between their premonitions and specific childhood events. About half the subjects had experienced an out-of-body experience. Half the sample considered themselves to be telepathic.

Of the 88 subjects, 85 completed the Eysenck Personality Inventory.[18] The results showed that the subjects were, overall, significantly more neurotic than the normal population. The result is double-edged. The greater neuroticism of the sample could perhaps mean that emotionality attunes the organism to the receptivity of premonitory information.

Indeed, the measure approaches statistical significance with both the accuracy and the number of premonitions. It might be argued too that the emotive nature of dreams could encourage premonitions. Certainly, many premonitions seem to have an emotional rather than an intellectual basis. On the other side of the coin, the higher neuroticism might be said by some to show that the accounts are likely to be exaggerated. (Figure 2)

The EPI results also revealed that the sample scored significantly higher on the 'Lie' scale than the normal population. However, the finding must be treated cautiously because the interpretation may be too simplistic. Basically, the EPI contains nine questions designed to see whether subjects are answering the questionnaire in an unrealistic fashion. However, the questions could also be seen as a sort of test of good social behaviour and whereas most of us score only averagely, some groups are more superior. The area needs more study.

The EPI test also measures extraversion-introversion. The sample was not significantly different from the normal population on this scale.

Looking at the types of premonition reported by this sample

Visions of the Future

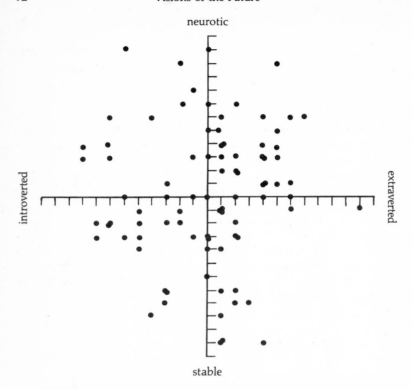

Figure 2 *Personality scores (Eysenck Personality Inventory) of 85 percipients. Percipients tend to be more neutrotic (over emotional) than most people.*

of subjects, slightly over half said that their premonitions were of more than one type. The largest category of premonitions was the dream (over four out of 10), followed by waking thoughts (nearly four out of 10), waking imagery (about one in nine) and sleep-onset imagery (one in 10). When asked to judge what proportion of their premonitions came true, nearly half said 90 to 100 per cent were fulfilled, a third thought 70 to 90 per cent were fulfilled, and the rest came true less than 70 per cent of the time.

The latency period between premonition and fulfilment was, in descending order of frequency, *days* in about three out of 10 subjects, *weeks* in slightly under three out of 10, *months* in a fifth, *hours* in slightly under a fifth, and *years* in four out of 100 subjects.

About six out of 10 of the participants had at some time warned someone in connection with a premonition.

One of the questions tried to find out how accurate premonitions are. Six out of 10 were self-judged to be very accurate, about a quarter were moderately accurate, one in 10 had some points correct, and four in 100 showed slight associations between premonition and later event.

Some subjects have premonitions on a particular theme. This was so with a quarter of subjects.

Being the 'receiver' of premonitions can affect people in different ways. Most subjects (over five in 10) were neutral in their attitude, but about three out of 10 subjects were unhappy with the situation and one in 10 were pleased to obtain future knowledge. Six out of 10 believed in life after death, a third were uncertain, and a small number (three out of 100) disavowed that notion.

Each subject was asked to provide at least one account of a premonition. On inspection it became clear that four basic themes could be readily identified: death (slightly over half the cases), unpleasant happenings (about a third), pleasant events (about one in 11 cases), and neutral things (one in 13 cases).

## Media-announcement premonitions

An analysis of premonition reports came up with a special subgroup which I have termed the media announcement type. They come in the form of radio or TV news items, newspaper pieces or placards, or any other form of public announcement, and are presumably hallucinated in some way. They seem very real and authoritative, but the content is premonitory. About one in 50 premonitions is of this variety. They might, and probably do go unnoticed as premonitions in many cases, until the percipient perhaps accidentally becomes aware subsequently that the broadcast event could not possibly have been known about at the time.

There have been several examples in this book. Perhaps the most amazing case was that of Lesley Brennan's foreknowledge of the Flixborough explosion. Others occurred surrounding the Kennedy assassination (Chapter 2). A few others have been mentioned too. Media-announcement premonitions seem to be especially accurate, and contain the essential facts about the later event.

'My daughter has had strange premonitions, and I write with her consent. About eight years ago she went to Greece for a holiday and, as her father was Greek, she was very impressed with the country and thought of little else over the next few weeks. One Sunday she came home from work and said that she had heard a newsflash on the radio saying that there had been a demonstration by Greek students and four had been shot dead. There was nothing in the papers about this for about a week, when it was reported as happening the previous day.

'We attached no importance to this as we thought that the news could have been suppressed for a time. The next incident happened later on a Saturday evening. Again she came home from work and told me that she had heard another newsflash. This time it was that the Greek government had been overthrown (this was the time when the colonels were in power), and the Greek people were free. I had just been watching the news and I know that anything of this importance would not have been omitted, so I telephone the BBC and asked for the newsdesk. I spoke to a man and asked him if there had been any such newsflash. He said "No". I have often wondered what that man must have thought afterwards. On Sunday morning, the next day, the headlines of the news were exactly what my daughter had told me the day before.'
MRS R. CAMBITSIS.

'I "hear" or "see" news broadcasts the day before they are really transmitted. One that is easily recalled began by listening to the 7 a.m. news on the clock/radio in bed. After hearing the news I said to my wife "Funny name for an East German agent Gunter Guillaume, sounds French". She had not heard this, but thought I was asleep. Midday TV news covered the item but not the name, neither did the evening news. On Monday at 7 a.m., the news came on the radio, word for word as in my premonition.

'Similar cases concerned the news of the death of the racing driver Graham Hill, and an accident to a little boy in Blackburn. In both cases I heard news items before they were actually announced.'
FRANK BOLTON.

The American parapsychologist W.E. Cox read my account of the Flixborough premonition (Chapter 4), which had been published in the Journal of the Society for Psychical Research, and was prompted to submit for publication a case that he experienced some years ago.[19] In 1968 he was working in his shop constructing a 'PK machine'. The radio was on, and at about 1 p.m. he heard an item about the death of a Baptist minister. A mail truck had collided with the minister's car. Cox heard the item a few more times that day. The following day Cox went to Durham N.C. and returned that evening, taking a taxi on part of the journey. The driver mentioned a terrible accident that had happened late the previous night. It involved a minister attending the Baptist State Convention. Cox was puzzled because he had heard the news several hours earlier.

The next morning Cox telephoned the radio station on which he had heard the news. They stated that they had only learned of the news at 11.30 p.m. and it was aired on their midnight newscast. The person killed was the Rev Dr Claude White of Raleigh, whose car had crashed at 9.50 p.m. on 2 October — but no mailtruck was involved. Reports of the death appeared in the newspaper on the next day.

Why should this form of premonition exist? We receive, via the media, much information that may affect us emotionally so perhaps it is not so unexpected that premonitions should be obtained in this way.

It seems likely that the percipient is in fact asleep briefly while watching or listening to a news broadcast, and replacing items with 'dreamed' ones having precognitive elements. The possibility arises that persons who have this type of premonition could be used as subjects in an experiment intended to increase the incidence of such episodes. If such subjects were greatly deprived of sleep and then made to watch a TV news programme, it may be that during the brief 'micro-sleeps' that are experienced with sleep deprivation, news-items might be hallucinations involving precognition. A list, given by the subject afterwards, of recalled news items might contain extra pieces and these could be artificially induced premonitions.

## Precognition and time

J.E. Orme conducted a useful study of the period between premonition and event, looking at 148 cases.[20] The interval varied from less than a day to over 20 years. Most premonitions occurred in close time proximity to the event, and there was a dramatic decline in number of cases as the time interval extended. When plotted on a graph the relationship between number of cases and time interval from premonition was markedly curvilinear.

Orme also plotted 33 cases of telepathy in a similar way, taking the interval to be from telepathic experience to confirmation. He found the same relationship, but on a shorter time scale. Most cases were confirmed within an hour. Overall, using combined data, a mathematical measure of the association between the two factors of interval and incidence was discovered to be extremely significant and highly unlikely to have come up by chance. They are strongly linked in some meaningful way.

Orme sees precognition and telepathy as communication between a future part of the organism and its present. The 'feedback' or confirmation of the event, precognitive or telepathic, is an essential element of the process. Interestingly, Orme pointed out an analogy between memory and precognition. Memory, too, conveys communication between the past and present state and the same kind of decline curves are obtained in simple experiments on memory where persons learn random syllables and then have to recall them. Orme views the brain and nervous system not as a storage unit but as a means for enabling the flow of information from past to present.

In this chapter some of the studies in the field of precognition have been simply described to give a comprehensive view of how the difficult topic is tackled by scientists. It will have been noticed that a main feature of experimentation into precognition, and all areas of parapsychology, is that the results are often not repeated when performed again. It is a highly anomalous state of affairs, since some individual experiments can statistically produce incredibly significant results. The pattern is grossly different from that of the physical sciences. Many scientists have therefore immediately presumed that because results are not clearly repeatable then any effects cannot really exist. But the situation may be greatly more complex than it seems on the surface.

At this stage the many theories about precognition need to be inspected.

# 6

# Excuses and Explanations

Explanations of premonitions are wide ranging. The scientifically ultra-cautious have a battery of theories which can indeed evaporate some cases, though they patently fail to cope with all aspects of precognition. Some workers believe that *something* of a parapsychological nature is happening in apparent premonitions but fall short of accepting that information travels back in time from the future, even to the point of hypothesizing the amazing abilities of some people to make considerable things happen at a great distance. Those theorists who have been forced to create revolutionary ideas by manipulating concepts of time.

The first set of theories tries to 'explain away' premonitions along normal lines:

## Excuses

### Inference
The definition of a premonition stated in Chapter 1 excluded events that might be inferred from information available in the present. There are several situations where it is possible to predict events in a manner which at first sight seem to give support to a precognitive interpretation. A closer examination, though, rapidly exposes these cases. It is an easy matter to foretell, say, that there will be a bad house fire in which several children die around Christmas time, simply by observing recurring patterns of behaviour linked to particular periods. Similarly, one can safely 'foretell' that there will be murders of political leaders in the Lebanon because that country is highly unstable and factioned. Clearly, in

any serious investigation, cases of simple inference have to be 'weeded out' from collections of premonitions.

## Coincidence

It is quite true that taking any *single* premonition it is conceivable that the correspondence between premonition and later event was coincidental — no matter how extremely unlikely that association may be. A general principle of uncertainty therefore exists concerning individual premonitions. The link just could have been that one in a billion chance. That is why patterns have to be looked for in premonition.

Professional parapsychologists are of course perfectly well aware that very strange links between variables can occur accidentally, and that some apparently remarkable coincidences prove not to be of such a nature when viewed statistically.

There are some topics which, superficially, seem to provide good examples of premonition but the probablity of sheer coincidence is so strong that they are of little value. Vague premonitions of plane crashes are not of great interest to the researcher into precognition because a large plane crashes somewhere every two weeks or so, therefore coincidence is a reasonable contender for an explanation. The information would have to be much more specific or some other characteristic, like a consistent latency period between premonition and event, would have to manifest that would be highly unusual.

If premonitions were characteristically one-off events then chance coincidence would be the prime candidate for disposal of the phenomena. But observations show that most people who report premonitions say they can give lots of personal examples. The statistical odds against the chance hypothesis then becomes astronomical, and it is necessary to expand scientific concepts to incorporate the new data.

## Preferential selection

Another line of attack the sceptics use is to assert that the premonitions reported by a percipient as having come true have been preferentially selected from a larger body of material, most of which did not attain fulfilment.

Again, of course, they are undoubtedly correct with some percipients. Anyone making a large number of random guesses about the future will have 'hits' on occasion, by chance. If only those cases are reported then the biased data can appear to be impressive. Here, the investigator relies heavily on the evidence of credible witnesses close to the percipient.

The more scientific method is to get percipients to send their premonitions, as soon as they occur, to the investigator, so that the charge of selectivity is scotched from the start. In practice though, there are often irritating little hindrances to such experiments. Percipients may be unwilling to write detailed accounts and send them off regularly, for any number of valid reasons.

In the one study performed in this way, using a subject who had reported many premonitions, the results were encouraging (See the account on Barbara Garwell in Chapter 4). This type of investigation is an essential part of further studies.

## Prodromic dreams

One of the ancient Greek ideas about some premonitions, supported by Aristotle, centred on the subtle idea that the future state of the percipient's body could be determined at an unconscious level. Thus, in cases where the percipient dreamed that they would succumb to some illness such an illness then transpired, the basis of the knowledge could have been bodily stimuli not yet perceivable to consciousness. These 'prodromic' (before running or warning) dreams would refer to a growing malady in symbolic or direct form.

Very early sensations associated with, say, lung cancer could underly a recurring dream of fire or suffocation. A direct dream of having lung cancer might also be experienced. A stark dream of a diseased lung might in later months or years look as if it had been premonitory, but would not have been so in reality. However, this type of foreknowledge is not in practice a very frequent variety. In fact, these dreams form a potentially very important diagnostic source of information and require further study in their own right. A possible prodromic dream in my own records was supplied by a woman who was pregnant at the time:

'I was in a car driven by my father. The boot was in the front (symbolic?), and there were children in the boot. I was afraid they couldn't breathe. My father got a crowbar to let the children out. I woke anxious and sweating.'

The next day the woman had a miscarriage, at three months.

## Self-fulfilling prophecies

Aristotle, while admitting that the core of premonition reports were inexplicable, sagely observed that premonitions could sometimes lead to their own fulfilment. In other words, if someone believes that something is going to happen to them they may unconsciously behave so as to bring about the event.

If someone dreams of falling from a ladder, it may be that in some people the dream becomes almost an auto-suggestion, so that the dreamer rationalizes and finds that some painting needs to be done requiring a high ladder . . . The depths of human psychology are really little understood so all sorts of possibilities exist in this region.

Purely psychological suggestion can have devastating effects on the body's functioning, too. A dream about one's future state of health — an improvement or deterioration — could come about by suggestion. Certainly, the 'placebo effect' is well known in medicine. Give patients an inert substance masquerading as a drug, saying it will alleviate their illness, and a sizeable proportion will report really feeling better! The opposite can apply too, so that someone can feel worse. There are, also, anecdotal accounts of Australian aborigines dying soon after being 'hexed' by bone-pointing from a fellow aborigine. If a person's belief system is so rigid that a symbolic act can take on the full import of a definite prediction of approaching illness or death, then these consequences might ensue in some people. At a lower level of effect it seems not unlikely that in some cases an accident might be unconsciously 'arranged', or a psychosomatic illness might occur, as 'precognized'. Here again though, the explanation applies to only a few cases from the overall collection.

## Symptoms

Reports of experiencing premonitions and other psychical phenomena are symptomatic of some psychologically abnormal conditions, although it must immediately be stated that the vast majority of percipients are definitely not ill. In some patients having temporal lobe epilepsy, for example, disturbances of memory occur, and there may be a strong erroneous conviction that something was known about before it happened. The cases do not usually stand up to scrutiny however.

Interestingly, in ancient times epilepsy was known as the 'divine illness' since sufferers having a fit were thought to have access to information from the gods. A modern experiment in precognition using epileptics as subjects would seem to be a sensible step in the progress towards a better comprehension of premonitions. It might be that epileptics do actually have a heightened sensitivity to premonitions during the considerable brain disturbances accompanying a seizure.

Schizophrenia is a severe mental illness which has several forms. Auditory hallucinations (often of accusative voices) and intrusive thoughts (perhaps bearing messages from other creatures on a distant planet) are characteristic features. The information may sometimes constitute what the patient believes to be premonitions.

Some theorists reject the idea that all cases of premonition can be discarded as explicable by normal means and are prepared to admit supernormal explanations. There is, however, a profound problem that must be taken into account. Before we deal with it let us just touch on the issues of fatalism, determinism and free will.

## Fatalism, determinism and free-will

If premonitions are genuine then they imply perhaps, at first sight, that everything is pre-planned and that they portray events lined up and ready to happen. We can occasionally foresee those events, but they are quite inevitable. That, essentially, is the viewpoint of fatalism. Fatalism says two things: firstly, that what will happen will happen, and secondly, that what will happen cannot be averted. The former statement, though, does not necessarily entail the latter. Because something will happen does not mean that it cannot be stopped using free will. And we have seen that in some cases of premonition avoidance has been successful.

Determinism is really of two varieties. One, 'universal' form, imposes the view that everything is predetermined and so free will cannot exist. The other, 'motivational' form, accepts that free will can be exerted on behaviour. Most philosophers agree that we do possess free will. Thus, the idea of life being like a fixed hand of cards already dealt is not acceptable. Future events can be averted. But, herein lies a puzzle.

## The enormous problem

We know that a CAUSE, by definition, precedes its EFFECT. The big stumbling block about premonitions is that in these cases the opposite appears to apply i.e. the EFFECT (information about an event — the premonition) comes in time before the CAUSE (the event itself). How can information about an event be received before the event has happened?

This 'backwards (or retrogredient) causation' is a philosophical impossibility in the world as we know it. The problem results in the 'intervention paradox'. That is, if you have a premonition, say, about an explosion, and you take steps to avert that explosion successfully, then what is there to produce information concerning the explosion? There is now no event about which to have a premonition.

It is at this point that the feint hearted might be tempted, suddenly and somewhat unscientifically, to jetison the steadily increasing body of evidence for precognition because the current ruling is that it cannot exist. However, because we cannot see a suitable framework to accomodate premonitions at this stage, we must not ignore the evidence that accumulates. Scientific caution is one thing but this is where scientific imagination must come to the fore.

The existence of supernormal foreknowledge does not fit into the scientific scheme of things today, but this anomaly might well suggest that our whole comprehension of the universe, science, and ourselves is, in a crucial way, profoundly wrong — just as in physics, awkward 'impossible' observations led necessarily to the emergence of revolutionary relativity theory and quantum theory. However, an even more drastic rethinking of concepts would be required to encompass premonitions. No one, however, philosopher or scientist, can say that we have such a complete knowledge of the universe that precognition is impossible. That would be just too arrogant and foolish.

## Simultaneous telepathy/clairvoyance

The first 'supernormal' explanation of premonitions does not in fact require any juggling of ideas about time or space. It is that the percipient receives, by telepathic or clairvoyant means, knowledge of a set of circumstances that will result in an event at a later time. So, a percipient might know from the mind of an engineer that a chemical plant was unsafe, or they might 'view' a faulty part of that plant and thereby be able to foresee the outcome. Many parapsychologists, even, baulk at the implications of true precognition and so tend to support this kind of theory.

Thus, the renowned parapsychologist Ian Stevenson prefers to comprehend precognition as a combination of extrasensory perception and normal inference. 'It is possible that the subject, by paranormal means, gains access to information from which, once it is available to him, he can infer the future course of events. The sum of his inferences is then projected in the form of visual or other images which he relates to the future'.[1]

Even so, Stevenson finds that two types of experience cannot be accomodated within his explanation. Firstly, the sort of premonition that refers to something years ahead and that subsequently comes true, secondly, the positive results in some precognition experiments where very complicated methods are used to ensure a genuinely random selection of targets.

There certainly is a large body of evidence to support the notions of telepathy and clairvoyance. In fact, most research in psi communication has been conducted in these fields. Many laboratory studies have come up with outstanding results in favour of the psi hypothesis, but characteristically, experiments are not routinely repeatable.

In real life situations reports of telepathy are extremely numerous. The phenomenon seems to be enhanced at moments of human crisis. So many cases tell of thought transference coinciding with death.

When the Society for Psychical Research was established in London in the last century, a vast collection of cases of telepathy was made by Gurney, Myers and Podmore. They published their findings in the monumental two volume 'Phantasms of the Living'.[2] The work documented hundreds of excellent personal accounts. The researchers, however, exhibited 'experimenter bias' in that they excluded cases of foreknowledge, which was considered at the time as a not very likely phenomenon. Nevertheless, precognitive cases kept presenting themselves, demanding recognition and investigation.

There are often great difficulties in deciding whether a psi experience was distinctly precognitive or simultaneous. The timing is of crucial relevance in classification. If something unexpected happened it is a matter of determining precisely when it occurred and how sudden it was in relation to the 'received' information. Some events, like an earthquake, might begin to take place long before the catastrophic climax. It therefore has to be assessed whether the information was available to anyone beforehand, so that the news could have reached the percipient telepathically, or, whether clairvoyant information would have been meaningful to the percipient.

## The psychobolie

Another type of explanation of premonitions in a physical universe, which does not conflict with the doctrine of the forward direction of time, is based on the possibility that the percipient might actually *cause* the later event using mind-over-matter PK.

Such a theory was postulated by Dr Angelos Tanagras in 1929.[3] Tanagras was a Greek who at different times had been a physician, admiral and psychical researcher. His thought-provoking contribution to the field of premonitions was the uncomfortable idea that a paranormal force might exist, which he termed the psychobolie, that was capable of making later events happen. Certain people, it was suggested, had the power to cause disasters by a conscious or unconscious wish. The psychobolie was a PK force which could operate at a distance to affect people or objects. The force might have a good or bad nature, depending on the attitude of the person involved; the 'percipient'. According to this viewpoint, premonitions consist not of a passive viewing of the future but the active construction of a future event in the mind of a gifted PK subject. The theme was portrayed dramatically in the film 'The Medusa Touch' in which actor Richard Burton played the role of someone who evinced an increasing ability to cause catastrophes.

There is evidence that observable PK effects do occur.[3,4,5] Some people, under strict conditions, have been observed to affect objects by will-power. One modern exponent of this phenomenon from the paranormal repertoire is the Russian woman Nina Kulagina.[6] The famous Soviet parapsychologist Leonid Vasiliev conducted experiments with her in the 1960s. Eventually several researchers, including a few from the West, were able to study her powers.

According to the testimony of witnesses, Nina has the rare capacity to move small objects weighing up to several hundred grams without touching them. Objects made of wood, glass, metal, or plastic can be made to move over a distance of tens of centimetres — usually in a sliding motion. More than one item can be transported at a time, and in different directions. Liquids too can be affected so that an ink blot is elongated into a line.

The force may extend over a certain area because if Nina concentrates on moving one object other items in the near vicinity are also set into motion, but to a lesser degree.

An easy task for Nina is to swing a compass needle by thought. In one study she stopped and started a pendulum several times. The pendulum was enclosed within a glass cylinder. Two researchers tested her with a table tennis ball suspended on a light spring, in a 10x10x10 cm clear-plastic cube with one open side facing Nina. The results were filmed.

The ball was made to swing like a pendulum and knocked against the side of the box vigorously. The spring was also seen to extend considerably so that the ball moved slowly along the floor of the cube. When Nina relaxed, the ball jumped back to its original position. Throughout these tests Nina made no physical movement herself.

On one occasion Nina moved the pans of a balance. Thirty gram weights were placed on each side. Nina succeeded in holding down one of them for several seconds. When another 10 g were placed on the higher pan it still did not descent. Nina can, apparently, levitate a small ball between her hands. In biological tests Nina has stopped a frog's heart beating. She can also affect humans physiologically, both positively and deleteriously. [7]

These are all simultaneous effects though, and there is no known evidence that Nina can make things happen at a distance in the future. And could such small forces cause something of the order of magnitude, say, as an earthquake? Another point is that when a large number of people precognize an unexpected disaster it is surely more believable than they received information about the event beforehand, rather that they should all suddenly decide to make the same unlikely event happen using PK forces.

While the psychobolie idea is an essential one, fitting into a definite theoretical niche, it is a last resort for those who accept foreknowledge but try desperately to keep the phenomenon within the constraints of conventional modern ideology.

### Space-time folds

It was proposed by the respected American parapsychologist Gertrude Schmeidler, that precognition could be explained by topological 'folds' in the space-time matrix.[8] Distant objects could in fact be close if such folding existed and communication might be conveyed by a short route, appearing to travel faster than the speed of light. The idea, though, is highly speculative.

### Sub-atomic particles

Some theorists have imagined that psi information might be conveyed backwards through time by sub-atomic particles. The positron was proposed as a likely candidate by Richard Feynmann, the American Nobel prizewinner.[9] He thought that the particle was an electron travelling in reverse time.

Mathematician Adrian Dobbs suggested that an as-yet undiscovered particle which he termed the psitron could fulfil the role.[10] The particles would intersect with delicately poised neurons in the brain of the percipient. However, the brain would have to possess some unique capacity to capture and detect these particles, which clearly would penetrate all other objects. The trouble here is that these ideas clash with the cause and effect barrier.

### Psi fields

W.G. Roll hypothesized a 'psi-field' which surrounds all objects and interacts with other fields.[11] He asserted that a mental act caused the psi field to act on 'known physical forces'. In less than convinced mood, the philosopher C.J. Ducasse commented drily that Roll's hypothesis of psi fields 'no more explains precognition than does the supposition that a watch has a tick explains its ticking'.

### The specious present

H. Saltmarsh, who analysed many accounts of premonitions, attempted to manipulate our concept of psychological time.[12] He said that consciousness must have a certain duration in order to perceive anything. This idea was already known as the doctrine of the 'specious present' and was the idea of the American psychologist William James. Chunks of consciousness overlapped to form a continuity. However, Saltmarsh thought that the specious present was much longer in duration than at an unconscious level, projecting far into the future as well as the past. In fact, the past and the future were, in a sense, the present. If information could break through from the unconscious to the consciousness, say via dreams, then the 'future' could be accessible.

While sounding plausible on the surface, the idea has been given short shrift by philosophers. The notion is contradictory since it has things both existing and not existing simultaneously. Professor Broad postulated a second time dimension going in the reverse direction to normal time to overcome that problem, but the explanation is still not satisfactory.[13]

## Multiple time dimensions

Aeronautical engineer John W. Dunne revived much popular interest in precognition in the 1930s with his book *An Experiment With Time*.[14] He postulated the theory that the past, present and future co-exist. The passage of time is illusory since we are displayed a sequence of 3-dimensional sections of a 4-dimensional universe. A second level of consciousness can, say in sleep, move backwards or forwards along the 4th dimension and so gain access to past or future information. Dunne described another dimension for time in that second consciousness to exist, and so on, to an infinite regression. Philosophers have not given much support to the idea. Hypothesizing other time dimensions does not in practice progress our understanding of precognition.

## Acausal theories

Some writers have put forward explanations of psi where there is no link between cause and effect. The most notable form of this type of theory is the *Sychnronicity* model proposed by Jung and Pauli in 1955, and which is applicable to precognition. It is a rather mystical concept and is difficult to convey, but we might say that mental events in the percipient may be reflected by physical events in the external world.[15] The macrocosm of the universe is mirrored in the microcosm of the percipient's mind. Racial archetypes (represented in images and symbols) of our 'collective unconscious' are involved in the process in an intermediary capacity. Thus, considering Swedenborg's vision of the great fire in Stockholm, Jung stated that 'The fire in Stockholm was in a sense burning in him too'. The two events, while not joined causally, arose from a common archetype and produced a 'meaningful coincidence'.

Reasoning things out about premonitions using the logic of

conventional 'common sense' also leads to a noncommittal acausality position. The major bold conceptual advances in science though, such as relativity theory, have transcended 'common sense'. A much more imaginative assault on the problem needs to be mounted by philosophers with a healthy disregard for old notions.

## Group mind
Several writers have posited the idea of a universal consciousness. William James was of the opinion that each individual consciousness was part of a cosmic consciousness, and that our apparent separateness may be revealed to be an illusion under certain circumstances, such as 'trance states'.

Frederic Myers proposed the idea that we are fragments of a larger subliminal Self, 'Liable to leakages and to occasional rupture', so permitting apparent psi.[16] In a similar vein, G.N.M. Tyrell thought that there are links between people at a subliminal level, and that communications are presented to consciousness via 'mediating vehicles' such as hallucinations, dreams and emotions.[17] H.H. Price believed that we have a 'collective unconscious' and that the mind has devised a repressive mechanism which inhibits psi communication between individuals normally, otherwise swamping would result.[18] Whately Carington thought that such a universal mind was also possessed by animal species.[19]

Presumably, precognition could be accounted for in such theories by the escape of information to the physical world from the all-knowing mind entity which would know what was soon to happen.

## Divine/demonic influence
Some persons of a fixed religious persuassion consider that premonitions are manifestations of a divine scheme of things and point to examples in the bible where 'angels' have conveyed future knowledge.

On the other hand, some religious followers believe that premonitions are 'the work of the devil' and therefore should not be investigated. It is hard to counter such views in persons committed to an unalterable belief system. The attitude, of course, stultifies scientific progress in the field.

## Functional premonitions
Several theories have been described which attempt to explain *how*

precognition works. This author has propounded some ideas as to *why* they should happen in a physical universe.[20] It's not an unreasonable hypothesis that precognition developed through evolutionary processes for the benefit of the species with the purpose to aid survival. It would have an 'adaptive function'. Premonitions could provide useful forewarnings of disasters so that avoidance behaviour could be initiated. This author, at one stage, proposed such an idea, called the Group Replenishment theory, based on the findings of a survey of percipients.

Firstly, it was noted that the great majority of percipients were female — a fact which suggests that premonitions have a special biological link with females, and in some cases the ability would appear to be genetically determined.

Secondly, there was the observation that premonitions most frequently warn of death or injury to close ones. This demonstrates that premonitions are not random glimpses into the future, but functional alarms potentially enabling avoiding action to be undertaken.

Thirdly, it was discovered that there was a negative correlation between the age at which subjects experienced their first premonition, and the number of offspring those subjects had subsequently had in life (looking at persons past child bearing age): i.e. in general, the earlier the percipient had her first premonition, the more children she had later in life. This curious link may of course have been a statistical quirk, but it might be interpreted to mean that those percipients who survived a catastrophe at a young age went on to be more fecund.

In conjunction, these findings might form a 'group replenishment' notion. It is probably best to consider the early development of man in explaining this notion. If a disaster such as attack, disease, flood, or whatever, were about to befall a group, a young female of that group might have a premonition and at least save herself. Subsequently, she would produce more offspring, so tending to make up the numbers of the group (group replenishment).

If the effect is genuine it is possible to hypothesize that the first sign of an impending large-scale disaster would be observable 'flight' behaviour, or psychosomatic behaviour, in young female percipients. They might 'go missing' or have slight accidents or illnesses.

One can speculate that the Greenham women, a group of women

who have doggedly camped outside Greenham Common and other
USAF bases in England as a protest against nuclear weapons, might
have been unconsciously precognizing a nuclear disaster such as
the Chernobyl catastrophe.

In a way, this type of theory seems logical and acceptable, but
there is still the intractable problem of the impossibility of
information travelling backwards in time. But, is there some other,
much deeper level of explanation?

The picture we have so far is of many disparate explanations
of foreknowledge. The 'explain-away' type cannot cope with very
many cases, and philosophical limitations seem to rule out many
superficially plausible supernormal explanations. If precognition
is totally incompatible with a materialistic world then the idea of
a purely mental state of affairs must be taken very seriously.

# 7

# Futures

## Credence

What credence can we give to accounts of premonition? There can be absolutely no doubt that the very great majority of cases, if not all, reported in this book are sincerely reported. The percipients showed much co-operation, providing detailed descriptions of their experiences and filling in questionnaires and personality tests. It was frequently commented by percipients that they were only too happy to help research and were pleased that a scientific interest was being taken into premonitions. The fact that some felt profound guilt about not warning victims demonstrates the definite association between premonition and later event in the mind of the percipients. In addition, the total *certainty*, so often reported about the future event, underlines the psychological impact of the experience.

Premonition reports bear the most rigorous examination. The three percipients who were studied in depth for Chapter 4 were perfectly able to substantiate their reports of foreknowledge by giving the names and addresses of credible witnesses. Signed statements were thus obtained, fully confirming the percipient's original description. Clearly, premonitions are not will-o'-the-wisp phenomena and they should be respected as valid data by laypersons and scientists alike.

Another factor which bolsters the reputation of premonitions is the unquestionable truth that they have been present throughout recorded human existence, regardless of the type of society or its belief system at the time. Their durability as a human characteristic is beyond question. They are, therefore, fully deserving of proper study like any other phenomenon that has been so enduring.

G.W. Lambert in 1965 listed several criteria which he considered essential for a premonition (he was concerned with dreams) to be taken seriously and scientifically:[1]

1.  The dream should be reported to a credible witness before the occurrence of the event to which it appears to relate.
2.  The time interval between the dream and the event should be short.
3.  The event should be one in which the circumstances of the dreamer seemed impossible at the time of the dream.
4.  The description in the dream should be of an event destined to be literally fulfilled and not merely symbolically foreshadowed.
5.  The details of the dream should tally with the details of the event.

The data from cases in this book may be compared with Lambert's desiderata. On the first point, while most of the accounts have to be taken on trust, the percipients who were singled out for close investigation constituted, in a sense, a 'spot check'. They produced, nevertheless, good cases where reliable witnesses were indeed informed before the fulfilment of the premonition.

As regards point two, a detailed analysis has been performed of the time interval between premonition and event in a sample of 50 cases. In nearly half (46 per cent), the latency period was one day or less and the frequency fell off sharply to a period of six days. Interestingly, however, there were later isolated peaks at seven, 14 and 21 days latency. These may have been due to percipients not being sure of the latency period and going for a round figure — a week, a fortnight and so on, but there is also the possibility that a psychological time rather than physical time is a factor in premonitions. In general, the curvilinear relationship between latency and frequency of premonitions is in agreement with that observed by Orme. Lambert's requirement is therefore met in most of these cases.

In fact, point three is a somewhat contentious criterion. Many premonitions are about things that happen within the routine of the percipient's lifestyle. Thus, a woman dreams that her mother will die on a specific day, and she does. The interest is in the accuracy of the premonition, the strength of its accompanying sense of conviction, and its pattern in relation to others experienced by the percipient. Nevertheless, some of the cases are certainly of the type specified.

Most premonitory dreams show in a clear visual manner what is to happen in the future, so nearly all cases conform to point four. However, we might quarrel with the criterion because it is unfairly dismissive of symbolic premonitions. They might be very important ones but they go unrecognized because the symbolism is not appreciated. Barbara Garwell's dream (page 66) of the 'SS man' shooting the ex-actor with the 'pockmarked face' is a very comprehendible symbolic reference to the assassination attempt on President Reagan. The premonitory nature of that dream was substantiated by its three week latency period; a repeating characteristic in some of Barbara's dreams. Symbolism is the very language of dreams therefore an area for possible investigation is just that symbolic premonitory dreams.

A large proportion of the premonitory dreams corresponded visually to the actual event really well (point five), to the extent that some percipients said that the premonition was precisely like the later event. In cases of public disasters the premonition was often said to be like an actual later TV report the percipient saw.

There is, then, considerable reason to believe that the premonition

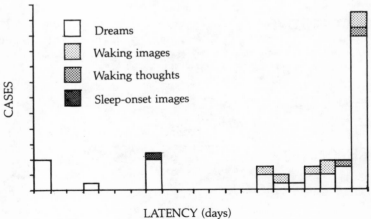

Figure 3. *Frequencies of latency periods (i.e. from premonition to event) in 50 reported premonitions.*

reports are acceptable, authentic data. The overall perspective, though, would be enhanced by a knowledge of the extent of public belief in precognition and its incidence.

Just how common is belief in foreknowledge in the population, and how many have really experienced the phenomenon? One study, carried out by Audience Selection in Britain in 1980, interviewed 896 people who were a representative sample of the population. Overall, approximately two-thirds (63 per cent) of those interviewed stated that they believed in dreams that came true. The figures were 69 per cent for females, and 56 per cent for males. In addition, 73 per cent of the sample believed in telepathy (79 per cent women, 67 per cent men). Roughly a quarter (26 per cent) had actually experienced such dreams (29 per cent females, 23 per cent males). Regarding telepathy, 29 per cent said they had personal experience.

Another survey, in Sweden in 1980, questioned 502 persons. Asked whether they believed that people could have experiences like premonitions and precognitive dreams, the findings were:

|  | Overall | female | male |  |
| --- | --- | --- | --- | --- |
| PREMONITIONS | 34% | 43% | 24% | 'Yes, absolutely.' |
|  | 35% | 35% | 35% | 'Yes, perhaps.' |
|  | 69% |  |  |  |
| PRECOGNITIVE DREAMS | 33% | 43% | 22% | 'Yes, absolutely.' |
|  | 38% | 34% | 42% | 'Yes, perhaps.' |
|  | 71% |  |  |  |

Those stating that they had experienced foreknowledge themselves provided the following results:

| PREMONITIONS | 21% | 26% | 17% | 'Yes, certainly.' |
| --- | --- | --- | --- | --- |
|  | 9% | 8% | 9% | 'Yes, perhaps.' |
|  | 30% |  |  |  |

These findings are deeply revealing.[2] They demonstrate that despite the current aloof attitude of current science, ordinary people with experience of real life accept the phenomenon. The fact simply cannot be brushed aside that over a quarter of all adults have experienced at least one premonition. That represents a truly vast number of cases. Clearly, in reality, no critic can deny that he or she knows no one close who has had a premonition. Percipients are far more common, say, than left-handed people. Premonitions are not a rare thing. They are a normal and natural component of life's events.

## Features

A comprehensive picture has been compiled of typical premonitions but a few aspects require comment. One straightforward but strong impression of premonitions is that they are, for the large part, parochial; concerning matters that are relevant in some way only to the percipient. They are about family and close ones very often. Some are about famous people but in this age when TV brings such people into our homes frequently a certain feeling of affinity can develop.

The foreknowledge has to be newsworthy to the percipient. It is thought that over half a million people died in an earthquake in Eastern China on 27 July 1976, but there does not seem to have been a spate of premonitions about the tragedy in the West. Presumably, there were cases locally.

Some premonitions concern, at least on the surface, people the percipient does *not* know. These are somewhat puzzling. Perhaps enough digging and probing might uncover links between percipient and victim in these cases, possibly revealing genetic relationships.

As we have seen, most premonitions are on unhappy themes. One fundamental consideration that could alter our view of premonitions as having a predominantly warning purpose is the matter of how many premonitions of a more neutral complexion are *not* reported to researchers. It is a potentially important factor because if most premonitions are trivial then theories of the function of precognition must shift their emphasis accordingly. There is a natural psychological bias to remember outstanding personal experiences of precognition, particularly if they forewarn of dramatic events. These cases are recounted more to oneself and others, and so become ingrained in memory. More frequently, excellent examples of precognition may be experienced but on far less exciting topics, so they will tend to be lost from easy access.

The under-reporting of 'neutral' cases is, then, probable.

We have to try to comprehend the significance of the various symbolic premonitory forms, such as omens, rappings and so on. They seem very different in kind from 'ordinary' types of premonition. So different, in fact, that they point to (and this is important) a dreamlike process operating in place of what we take to be reality. These cases might be said by some to be PK effects working with backwards causation, but the phenomena display great intelligence in their cryptic messages. They are uncomfortable to some parapsychologists, being just too much to have to explain. However, they must not be ignored. They just might hold the key to the mystery of foreknowledge.

There are no experiments in parapsychology that can be conducted time and time again and demonstrate a clearly repeatable effect. Of course if that were possible psi would now be a major area of psychology rather than 'para' (beyond, beside). Critics have naturally pointed to this truth to dismiss the whole area as one based on non-existent phenomena. A more thoughtful consideration, though, treats such total condemnation with considerable caution. There could well be valid reasons for the variation in experimental results.

Individual results can be staggeringly successful, with odds of hundreds of millions to one against chance. These studies cannot be ignored. They give considerable evidence of psi effects operating at the time and place of the experiments. Psi appears to be sensitive to certain human variables, such as the attitude of the experimenter as well as the subject. Complex psychological factors could affect the outcome of an experiment.

Even in orthodox psychology, especially social psychology, many well-known effects do not always manifest themselves in experiments. Some variable or other must be affecting the situation negatively on those occasions. In treating psi with the full vigour of experimental psychology techniques, no allowance is made for any delicacy or flightiness on the part of psi. We have seen how emotion is an integral component of many premonitions. In the clinical laboratory setting it seems remarkable that any evidence whatsoever of precognition can be uncovered!

## Questions and speculations

With so many observations and ideas abroad there is much scope for speculation about what is really happening when foreknowledge is manifested. A number of basic questions need to be tackled:

1. Where is the precognitive horizon? How far into the future can a percipient 'see'? There is undoubtedly a rapid drop-off effect in latency (the period between premonition and event) so that few premonitions foretell of events years ahead, but is there an absolute limit?

2. Is there a relationship between accuracy of the premonition and the latency period to fulfillment? i.e. Does the premonition become distorted or degenerated in some way (like memory) over reverse time? In memory experiments the most recently learned items are recalled best. In premonitions, are those closest to the event more accurate?

3. If an event is avoided by deliberate action does the event become displaced elsewhere by some law of conservation or compensation?

4. Are there cases where many people precognized an unannounced disaster? i.e. Can premonitions occur in the absence of feedback? Are there cases where the percipient had a premonition but died before it was fulfilled? (Long term prophecies such as those of Nostradamus have been too vague, and those associated with rigid belief systems are dubious). Assuming that feedback might cease or be interrupted at death, is there a 'pre-death precognitive pause' in gifted subjects which presages death?

5. Are there any links between the percipients when many people precognize an event? Are there, say, personality consistencies and are the percipients limited to certain geographical areas?

6. Does the number of percipients depend on the magnitude of the disaster?

Much painstaking work will have to be conducted to obtain answers to these important queries.

There is one aspect of premonitions, which I have observed in my own little experiences, that I believe could be of major significance. I can recall two precognitive dreams from years ago because I made notes at the time. In one, the antecedent situation was that I had watched a film on TV which included a scene showing musicians walking about in pub playing instruments. There was a good female pianist and a clarinetist. They played Gershwin's *Rhapsody in Blue*.

That night, I had a vivid dream of my daughter Katherine playing an instrument like a clarinet. I said to people in the dream, 'It's amazing, she's only one!' The next day an arts programme on TV (The Great Art Collection) mentioned a painting showing a little boy playing a similar instrument. The commentator stated, 'He couldn't be more than one.' The correlation struck me forcibly at the time, but the theme of the apparent precognition was not memorable subsequently.

On another occasion, one Friday night many years ago, I was attending a college studying 'A' level zoology. We were dissecting the dogfish, concentrating on the branchial basket (the cartilages in the gill region). Of the seven cartilages, numbers four and five are fused. The next night (Saturday), I had a vivid dream that I opened a newspaper and saw the football results listed. The first seven scores were all draws, except numbers four and five. It was obvious to me that there was a compelling association between the pattern of scores and the cartilage arrangement that I had been studying. Technically, the experience might not have been precognitive since the games had already been played when I had the dream. I had not known of the scores on the Saturday.

It is of very great interest to note that both dreams were based on a conceptually similar schema that was established just before the precognition. It must be considered seriously whether premonitions can only occur if there exists such a conceptual basis which, somehow, sensitizes the percipient to receive knowledge about the later event. It might also explain why some events are precognized and others are not. A suitable groundwork has to be present.

Pondering the subject of premonitions can generate many interesting and complex possible scenarios about their cause and operation. It is illuminating, even knowing the philosophical objections to foreknowledge, to indulge in a little speculation. Suppose that it was in fact possible for information to travel backwards in time by some undiscovered way. Let us consider the problem of how the inevitable event, by the unassailable law of cause and effect, could still provide a warning but would *not* result in the event being averted — therefore, the Intervention Paradox need not be invoked.

A sort of Theory of Selective Precognition develops. A law of selectivity would have to apply in that the information would only be received by persons who would not be capable of bringing about avoidance of the main event. Backwards travelling information would travel via 'safe' routes of 'non-influence' i.e. those pathways which would not result in avoidance. The notion of Influential and Non-influential percipients arises. The former, who could stop an event, would not be subject to precognition about a disaster, whereas the latter might receive extremely accurate foreknowledge. Peripheral avoidance might occur i.e. persons who were not in a position to avert the main event might avoid the disaster personally, by taking appropriate action.

The main event would therefore be self-limiting to some extent in that the greater the disaster, perhaps the more peripheral avoidance or if the event is favourable, the more people would benefit. This model, however, begins to get unwieldy and convoluted when one thinks about how non-influential percipients are selected. The theory begins to look like a 'divine intervention' explanation.

Another line of thinking concerns the problem of the Intervention Paradox. Because of man's powers of imagination and comprehension, an averted event could have as much impact on people's minds as an actual event. To avert an event, it might be said, is not to abolish subsequent cognitive/emotional responses in persons to the averted 'potential' event. In other words, it might be argued that although an event might be averted by acting on a premonition, there would still be 'vicarious responses' in persons later when they reflected on what might have occurred. These vicarious responses could be identical to the responses to an actual event. Thus, the physical event itself would be of no relevance in the premonition, rather the significant element would be the psychological response of people to that event. Both these ideas are stated to show how one has to approach precognition, but they remain essentially unsatisfactory.

## Levels of understanding

The world in which we live has a sense of solidity and permanence, and in our everyday existence we are emotionally and intellectually reassured by routine and predictability. We all want to feel safe and secure.

But just let us inspect four random people. Firstly, take an engineer. His perception of the world is considerably reinforced by his observations nearly all the time. If the force on this piece of metal is so much then the movement here is that much . . . In his work simple cause and effect is confirmed to him for the millionth time. He may use a computer to solve complex mechanical problems. Its total reliability is taken for granted. He can build a rocket that will reach the moon.

Now, look at a nuclear physicist conducting an experiment with a particle accelerator. He can demonstrate that time actually passes slower on fast moving particles. He also has to contend with the fact that he cannot state certainly where an electron is at any one moment, moving round a proton. There are some unknowable things.

Now consider a psychologist studying visual perception. He can show that people grossly misperceive objects and persons in certain situations. Literally, we cannot always believe what we see. Our perceptions are affected by all manner of factors, including attitude. The psychologist's understanding of the world must incorporate the notion that weird distortions of what is normally termed 'reality' can occur in everyone.

Finally, look at the parapsychologist whose everyday thoughts are on such things as action happening without any known force, knowledge being acquired of an event before that event happened, and other 'impossible' but reported phenomena.

It is immensely difficult for people used to the unchanging action-reaction experience of life to accept that there are aspects of existence characterized by strange inexplicable and uncertain phenomena. A law of increasing uncertainty seems to apply the more one looks into matter and mind.

A person solely experiencing the engineer's frame of reference may claim to be living in the 'real' nuts and bolts world, but he is not comprehending the true world. The perspective is far too narrow. Most scientists operate within the engineer's domain so, understandably, some of the notions of parapsychology are viewed as subversive, threatening to demolish their carefully constructed models. But if we are to seek a better understanding of ourselves and the universe we must look far beyond the terribly simple but deceptive 'reality' that ordinarily confronts us. The most upsetting idea to traditional science is that it has been labouring under a great delusion i.e. that the physical universe actually exists. But what if there is no physical matter. What if life is, in a sense, a Great Dream?

The thought had occurred to ancient Chinese philosophers:

'While men are dreaming they do not perceive that it is a dream. Some will even have a dream within a dream. And so when the great awakening comes upon us, shall we know this life to be a great dream. Fools believe themselves to be awake now!'

Chinese sage, Chuang Tzu

Shakespeare referred to the idea:

'We are such stuff as dreams are made on, and our little life is rounded with a sleep.'

The Tempest

In Western philosophy the concept of non-materialism has been known as Idealism and was particularly propounded by Bishop Berkeley.[3] Samuel Johnson rejected the idea somewhat histrionically, and with uncharacteristic lack of insight, by kicking a stone saying 'I refute it thus', but of course he had not.

The Oxford philosopher H.H. Price wrote in 1949:

'We must conclude, I think, that there is no room for telepathy in a materialistic universe. Telepathy is something which ought not to happen at all if the materialistic theory were true. But it does happen. So there must be something seriously wrong with the materialistic theory, however numerous and imposing the normal facts which support it may be.'[5]

That argument is even more potent when we consider the immense anomaly of precognition, which is philosophically quite incompatible with a physical universe. In fact, all the psi phenomena can be accommodated much more readily in a purely mental scheme of things. It seems a preposterous suggestion. How does one come to such a conclusion, and what testabled hypotheses could be proposed?

There is a special type of dream which is so incredible, that anyone having experienced it cannot help but question what we assume to be 'reality'. It is known as a 'lucid' dream. This is where the dreamer becomes perfectly aware, while asleep, that he or she is dreaming. It is much more than just a vivid dream. You become conscious, just as you are when awake, and you *know* that your body is really in bed but that the situation in which you find yourself is a clever construction of your mind.

It is a puzzling concept to understand if you have never had a 'lucid' dream. The phenomenon is rare in most people, although some individuals dream lucidly every night.

I was able, for the first time, to get lucid dreamers to signal out information to the world of wakefulness when lucid, by making coded eye movements. The rest of the body's musculature is inhibited in dreaming sleep.

The sudden transformation of an ordinary dream to a lucid dream happens usually when some glaring inconsistency or anomaly is noticed, so 'triggering' the state. The anomaly may, for instance, be seeing someone who is dead, or some other impossible event:

'My sister showed me a vase she had found. She dropped it and after breaking into tiny pieces it became whole again. I realized something was not right. I then knew I was dreaming.'

Even curiouser, another characteristic is that you can control events in the dream by mere thought. A specific person may be made to appear or the location may be altered. You possess superhuman abilities, like being able to walk through walls, or 'fly':

'I said to myself, "I don't like this, it's only a dream anyway and I'm going to change it". I had a feeling of utter confidence and I smugly produced not only a suitcase full of money, but also a private aeroplane with a crew and a personal attendant.'

It is a memorable experience to be in an exquisitely detailed dream setting and question a dream character whose answers are intelligent and perfectly logical. The lucid dreamer may decide to conduct experiments within the dream:

'I dreamt that I stood at a table before a window. On the table were different objects. I was perfectly aware that I was dreaming and I considered what sorts of experiments I could make. I began by trying to break a glass, by beating it with a stone. I put a small tablet of glass on two stones and struck it with another stone. Yet it would not break. Then I took a fine claret glass from the table and struck it with my fist with all my might, at the same time reflecting how dangerous it would be to do this in waking life; yet the glass remained whole. But lo; when I looked at it again after some time it was broken. It broke all right, but a little too late, like an actor who misses his cue. This gave me a very curious impression of being in a fake world, cleverly imitated, but with small failures.'[6]

Even in the dream world there are certain internal 'laws of physics' that operate. I was fortunate to discover the first consistent effect in dreams — the 'light-switch' phenomenon. If you attempt to switch on a light in the dream scenery, something prevents it happening. Whatever produces the dream tries to get round that essential limitation of not being able to cope with a sudden increase in imagery — brightness, by, say, making it look as if the light bulb has fused or that the switch is faulty. The dream strives to fool the dreamer and maintain a pretence:

'I switched it on and off several times and looked up at the light, which was a naked bulb. It kept sparking and flickering, I could see the filament light up and glow orangey-red. I thought, 'Typical of this place, nothing works properly.'

When reflecting on the phenomenon during wakefulness the question naturally comes to mind, is waking life an even more carefully construed and plausible yet actually deceptive dream? The term 'dream' here is not perhaps exact, because it implies that there exists a solid, tangible world in which one eventually awakes. It would seem more likely that all existence is an illusion, including 'death' and beyond.

Is there a corresponding 'lucidity' that can be achieved concerning what we take to be true 'wakefulness'? Once the notion is established, niggling questions about the 'true world' begin to present themselves.

There are flaws in the dream world that enable the lucid dreamer to recognize that the situation is not that of wakefulness. The verisimilitude of the dream setting with wakefulness is so complete that sometimes a decision is not easy! Skilled, habitual lucid dreamers have a checklist of little tests to perform to ascertain their current state.

Just as there are flaws in the dream world that enable the knowledgeable dreamer to become aware of the actual situation, are there flaws in the 'real' world of wakefulness to indicate that everything is not what it seems? The answer, actually, is in the affirmative.

The very phenomena of parapsychology — PK, telepathy, precognition, etc., do not fit into the materialist idea of things. They occur like errors in the huge deception. Thus, we can contemplate the uncomfortable possibility that the whole universe is a fake.

There is another phenomenon of dreaming that adds to the puzzle. It is termed the 'false awakening'. Occasionally one may *dream* that one is awake. What might happen is that you think you have woken. Everything is precisely as it should be. You get up, wash, have breakfast, but then you might look out of the window and notice that the street outside is not your street! You then awaken. Some people report having had multiple false awakenings, leaving them very confused. Inevitably we must ask, as did the Chinese sage, whether there is yet to be another awakening at 'death'. In such a scheme there might well be strange conceptual associations resulting in synchronization, premonitions and the like in the Great Illusion process.

The idea of a mind world is immensely provocative and impertinent to science, but what testable hypothesis can be deduced? There are some possible consequences of the idea. If life is a clever and intricately constructed illusion in which we all share, then everything else — the entire universe — is part of that illusion.

In that case, the extent of the progress of the dream is here and now, at this second. From that fact it follows that we shall never make contact with intelligences in space that are more advanced than us. They might be at an equal or more primitive stage of knowledge, but never beyond.

That constitutes a view which is opposed to the view of modern materialistic science. The belief is that there are vast numbers of alien species at a more sophisticated stage of development. Some physicists however are beginning to wonder when they are going to make themselves known. Any contact in fact would tax the illusion process very considerably!

Another hypothesis the notion suggests is that we shall never quite be able to reach an understanding of the nature of matter at the sub-atomic level, because the Great Illusion will always introduce something to protect its basic monumental deceit. Although, as we see, it may have been compromised!

These ideas are mind-boggling and may be hopelessly wrong, but I contend that we have to expand our thinking along such paths if we are to advance real science. At this time man's knowledge of himself and the universe is, quite honestly, puny.

### Future avenues

A research technique that will be most valuable in future studies of real life premonition cases is certainly the collection of premonition reports that are deposited with an independent person immediately on 'reception' by the percipient. The study with Barbara Garwell gave results that greatly encourage further work. The method overcomes all sorts of criticisms that can be levelled at post-hoc accounts.

In addition, further large-scale case collections would be useful from different countries for cross-cultural analysis. Of course, many more individual cases also require full investigation to increase the data base of authenticated cases. Rather deeper probing of gifted percipients might determine whether the 'conceptually similar pre-premonition experience' is a consistent feature that could aid theorizing.

From experience I knew that the snag about getting subjects constantly to fill in reports and send them back to the experimenter is that the procedure gets to be tedious for percipients. It is an understandable attitude when the percipient is usually unpaid and any feedback about the study is certainly not immediately available. The period from the start of a study to actual publication may be a few years.

The answer, I believe, is to pay percipients a reasonable amount for their full co-operation in premonition research. This could add up to a fair sum if a large sample is to be used, but such funding is essential for proper research.

If the material world is a great illusion and everything is a mental construction then we should not be surprised to encounter strange associations between theoretically independent events. With this in mind, we should re-assess the old ideas of foreknowledge. In the ancient world omens, for example, were of popular interest and their symbolic warning had to be skilfully interpreted. We think nowadays that surely such ideas were just silly superstition with no basis in fact. It would be as well, however, to rid our minds of *all* bias and re-investigate such phenomena in the light of modern knowledge. Omens would be compatible with a 'mind world'.

A detailed collection of cases of modern omens would be a valuable contribution to science. Consistencies might be discovered that would assist a deeper understanding of the phenomenon. Just one example that springs to mind concerned the tragic space shuttle disaster which killed seven US astronauts in January 1987. There were several postponements of the flight, but what caused the final one was that the shuttle's hatchdoor inexplicably would not close. It was a peculiar little incident over which people just shrugged their shoulders but what would an ancient oracle have made of it? An omen, surely. Omens are a variety of premonition in symbolic form — they deserve more investigation.

Another area to re-examine is the ancient notion that an innate capacity for precognition could be exercised just before death. Both Plato and Aristotle were of the opinion that it was possible.

We know that all sorts of anomalous phenomena surround death, such as deathbed visions and telepathic experiences. Perhaps here too, the ancients were aware of human abilities that go unrecognized today.

It goes without saying that any experimentation in the field would be difficult to carry out for several ethical reasons, but it is not too impossible to imagine that some co-operative persons near death, wishing to advance science, might participate in serious experiments in precognition.

The persistent stories of lights appearing before death, such as 'corpse candles', are greatly intriguing. They may be 'psychic' lights, seen only by sensitives, but they, might be a physical phenomenon which could be much more readily sensed using modern electronic equipment. The anecdotal evidence suggests that optical monitoring of deathbeds would produce inexplicable readings before death, even if the lights were invisible to the naked eye. Other regions of the electromagnetic spectrum could also be studied in the same situation.

The renowned method of future-seeing by scrying, in all its form, is another area that urgently calls for re-enquiry.

From the mind world viewpoint, any of the techniques for seeing into the future employed in ancient civilizations might turn out to be workable. There can be no argument that those practices declined not for lack of interest or efficacy but because of heavy-handed suppression by the church, and simplistic early science. We may be quite surprised by the effectiveness of those procedures if resurrected today. Techniques that were refined over millenia should not be haughtily ignored.

### Premonition induction

Some of the findings about premonitions, considered together, lead to the speculative suggestion that it might be feasible to induce premonitions in some people artificially. One of these is the observation that an exaggerated emotional state is often an important factor associated with the premonition, both at fulfilment and 'reception'. At the moment of 'feedback' (i.e. when news of the event is received), many percipients respond with great emotionality, perhaps sobbing uncontrollably, because the premonition is taken so personally. Percipients can feel very guilty for not warning victims. At the time of having a premonition many percipients are in an emotional upheaval. That the percipients are generally emotional is confirmed by the EPI results (page 91).

The emotional element is also of relevance in other psi situations, from telepathy, where some remarkable cases are linked with personal crisis, to poltergeist cases, where emotionally disturbed teenagers seem to be an important component. In voodoo practices, deliberate emotional driving is part of the build up ritual.

The second aspect to consider is the vehicle for premonitions. The dream is the major source, but the dream state itself may not be 'special' for psi production. The heavy bias of dream premonitions may be misleading. It is conceivable that a premonition is triggered when a random image or thought happens to coincide with the later event. In dreams many diverse images are produced so the likelihood of a tie-up is greater. The implication is that if percipients indulged in increased day dreaming, say, or creative writing, more premonitions would ensue. This author's personal observation that premonitions seemed to be founded on an event that happened a day or two before the premonition, and which was conceptually similar, supports that idea.

Modern technology might be employed to increase both the seemingly crucial elements of emotionality and random imagery so as to facilitate premonitions in gifted subjects. The result might be a workable 'premonition machine'!

## Unscience

'Educated people know that premonitions are impossible. Now that science has satisfactorily answered so many questions concerning nature and the universe, and indeed has got us to the moon, why should we bother with these irritating accounts of people claiming to know what will happen in the future? Furthermore, who are these foolish parapsychology people who seem intent on upsetting the scientific applecart? They must of course rank with flat-earthers and cranks who communicate with diminutive chartreuse-hued entities from the planet Mars. Of course we don't find it necessary to read any of their papers on the topic — we musn't encourage these misguided people. All right, my aunt Jane said she knew that uncle Joe was going to die in that freak accident, but that must have been a coincidence. Naturally, I do not discuss premonitions with colleagues, they'd think I was insane. I would consider anyone mad who talked to me on the subject in a less than critical fashion.'

Those composite sentiments represent the attitudes of many people at this time who, conditioned to a simple cause and effect view of events and by prevailing viewpoints, cannot conceive of any other scheme of things. Among the 'impossiblists', scientists themselves are probably the worst offenders. Because a scientist may be an expert in one narrow field of enquiry, he has no automatic ascendancy over non-scientists when discussing a different area. His opinion may be as weighty, or perhaps less, than that of any lay person. Unfortunately, science is full of pompous, arrogant people who bluff their way through when discussing things they hardly know anything about. Worse, non-scientists tend to place too much credence on the utterances of such scientists. They unwisely assume that they must be better informed than themselves.

Many scientists seem not to be aware of the wholly unscientific stance they take regarding parapsychology. It is a cardinal error to an experimenter to deliberately ignore a body of data. Such biased sampling would completely invalidate any experiment and attract justifiable censure. Yet in their assessment of premonitions very many 'scientists' do precisely that. They disregard information and conform to current biases. The result has been that an area of fundamental importance has suffered neglect, and our comprehension of the nature of all things has possibly been distorted.

In any other field of scientific endeavour anomalous findings would be grasped and investigated thoroughly, since they often indicate that the current theory is inadequate in some way. Consistent cases of reported premonition, telepathy and other psi effects are studiously ignored. In many psychology departments at universities, totally trivial and wasteful researches have been tolerated for years, yet profound experiments in parapsychology have not even been considered out of sheer unreasoned bias.

To illustrate the almost unbelievable bias in psychology against parapsychology, in Britain, here are just 3 remarks (from many) made to me by psychologists:

On visiting one department and mentioning my research into parapsychology the Professor, to whom I was talking, almost visibly recoiled, stating proudly 'We're a very hard-nosed department here' — as if somehow my years of scientific training in experimental psychology were not applied to that work.

My main laboratory research has centred on sleep and 'lucid' dreaming. One sleep researcher, on the air, stated 'There has been some work done on 'lucid' dreams, but it has been performed by people interested in parapsychology.'

Another Professor, again on air, said 'I don't see why I should take into account ESP in my work.'

Many areas of orthodox psychology are, in truth, highly suspect. Some people have made reputations and gained high office on work that has not subsequently matched the original results. The area of 'hypnosis' has been shot to pieces in recent years by careful research. It was amusing to me that the 'star hypnosis subject' of one vehement critic of parapsychology and researcher into 'hypnosis', informed me that she never was in any kind of 'trance' in his experiments. It was purely a case of social compliance with a dominant experimenter who was unscientific enough not to recognize the true psychology of the experimental situation. If a researcher can be so blind about his own field, he is hardly in a position to castigate other areas.

Psychology's unfairness is not, strangely, a unique situation. Psychology went through a particularly psychotic episode during the 'Behaviourism' period, following the eccentric and simplistic code of J.B. Watson that only things that could be physically observed should be studied. Major areas such as imagery, dreams, mind, and consciousness disappeared from the literature and the lips of psychologists for decades in that time of academic repression. Eventually, having become warped and stunted, psychology struggled free of that self-imposed strait jacket.

Why is science so implacably antagonistic to parapsychology?

There are several reasons. A major one, I believe, actually goes back to the Middle Ages when the official Christian Church condemned phenomena that form the subject matter of modern parapsychology as being 'sorcery'. That was despite the fact that foreknowledge, say, formed an essential part in the development of Christianity. Dream incubation was practised in churches in England up to the Middle Ages. That blanket suppression not only stifled the practice in and knowledge of these topics, but also set them up as being anti-God — a powerful sledgehammer! Religious bigotry can persist for centuries and still exists today. It was influential in the last century when scientific parapsychology was emerging.

Another movement against parapsychology was the result of the Age of Reason, which progressed basic physical sciences tremendously, but undoubtedly threw the baby out with the bath water as regards more subtle aspects of life and nature.

Sheer academic ignorance is a further reason why anti-parapsychologism is maintained. It is an area contained under the broad umbrella of psychology, but few psychologists know anything about it at all. The topic is not taught in degree courses. In the presence of such dangerous ignorance there is also a disdaining attitude that parapsychology is somehow 'unscientific'. Most psychologists, though, have never seen a parapsychology journal so have no idea of the high level of experimentation. Anyone wishing to 'get on' in psychology does not make positive statements about parapsychology. The attitude is, alas, self-perpetuating. Those in authority who pronounce negatively on the subject would not have got to their place of eminence if they had ever supported the topic. No one dares step out of line, especially now that many psychology departments are in decline and some may be near possible demise.

In one way, however, parapsychology has given ammunition to its critics. The few cases of experimenter fraud have been regrettable, yet they tend to be cited with disproportionate emphasis by critics. Fraud, of course, exists just as much in orthodox psychology. A whole area must not be written off because of the foolish behaviour of some researchers.

Finally, a powerful reason for scientists not smiling upon parapsychology is that it is seen as potentially capable of undermining their whole idea of science. No scientist wants his or her life's work to be evaporated, or made questionable. The loss of face and esteem would be too painful. Parapsychology though is providing a medicine that will have to be taken by science.

The public's attitude to science is greatly affected by scientific journalism. In some key publications — magazines, newspapers, radio, TV, — those in power have a negative attitude to the paranormal. Consequently, the public remain in the dark about advances made in the field. Fortunately, some of the popular press, which know that people experience premonitions and want more information, prevent the topic from being totally taboo.

Many 'scientific' journals have a disgraceful attitude to parapsychology and completely reject and suppress any publications of that type. Future generations will find such thinking incredible.

### Conclusions

It will be clear by now that the understanding of precognition is not an easy matter. It is possible to concoct notions of *why* precognition might be present in a physical universe, and certain evolutionary ideas come readily to mind, but all such theories come tumbling down when confronted with the cause and effect problem using the very philosophy of a physical universe.

At this juncture there are really two alternatives. Firstly, to backtrack and suddenly find fault with all the hundreds of millions of premonitions that have been experienced and try to stuff all the evidence into the limited container of materialism, or, to take a deep breath and face the probability that since the phenomena exist, then materialism must be erroneous — that life is in a sense a cunningly contrived 'dream'. We seem to be propelled in that direction by the facts. Conan Doyle's character Sherlock Holmes put it plainly:

> 'How often have I said to you that when you have eliminated the impossible, whatever remains *however improbable,* must be the truth?'
> *The Sign of Four,* Sir Arthur Conan Doyle.

There is no doubt that a mind-state universe is capable of accepting all the peculiar phenomena studied by parapsychologists, not to mention all the inexplicable phenomena and beliefs of the various religions.

We should start to theorize more along the line that we share an existence in a mind universe. It need not be an unprovable assertion. The system is logically structured but with findable 'errors'. My own hypothesis about not ever communicating with more advanced species is just one that could indicate the likelihood of the Great Dream theory. There must be other testable hypotheses. We have now to search for clues and flaws in the Great Dream. We could look for examples of visual and conceptual 'puns' in the universal construction, just as in nocturnal dreams. There must be limitations to the capacity and ingenuity of the Great Illusion process that could be revealed.

One intriguing question is what would happen if it could be demonstrated that the theory was correct? On reflection it seems that probably nothing would alter physically, in that the system has a strong, well-established logical foundation, so its laws and structures would remain as before.

There would, however, be a massive change of attitude in people about their personal destiny. If life is a dream-like experience, then consciousness can survive 'death' and enter some other dream. Religious thinking would predominate, considering especially the matter of to what extent one's present life-style affects the next illusion. The world would be transformed.

There would be a great turning away from materialism and a developing interest in spirituality and mysticism — a far cry from the current outlook on life in Western society.

The judgement on 'Science' of the nineteenth and twentieth

centuries in the long term may well be castigated for its extreme narrow-mindedness, compartmentalization, absurd reductionism, and unscientificness in steadfastly ignoring the parapsychological data. In materialistic terms, many present day scientists are like ants exploring a computer, the significance of which totally escapes their comprehension. The unpalatable fact to orthodox science is that it may simply be discovering the rules of operation of various little subsystems, like the rules that exist in a nocturnal dream. It is, nevertheless, a dream.

# Reference Lists

**Chapter 1**
1. McKeller, P. (1957) *Imagination and Thinking* Cohen & West, London.
2. de Becker, R. (1968) *The Understanding of Dreams* George Allen & Unwin, London.
3. Dodds, E.R. (1971) Supernormal Phenomena in Classical Antiquity. *Proceedings of the Society for Psychical Research (Procs. S.P.R.)*, Vol 55, pt 203 March, pp 189–237.
4. Cheetham, E. (1973) *The Prophecies of Nostradamus* Corgi Books, London.
5. Aubrey, J. (1696, reprinted 1890) *Miscellanies*. Library of Old Authors, Reeves & Turner, London.
6. Sidgwick, H. (1888) On the evidence for premonitions. *Procs. S.P.R.*, 5: 288—354.
7. Pauli, H. (1966) *The Secret of Sarajevo*. Collins, London.

**Chapter 2**
1. Rhine, L.E. (1955) Precognition and Intervention. *Journal of Parapsychology*, 19 (1): 23.
2. Ibid: 17.

**Chapter 4**
1. Hearne, K.M.T. (1982) Three Cases of Ostensible Precognition from a Single Percipient. *Journal of the Society for Psychical Research (J.S.P.R.)*, 51 (791): 288–291.
2. Hearne, K.M.T. (1986) An Analysis of Premonitions Deposited Over One Year From An Apparently Gifted Subject. *J.S.P.R.*,

53 (804): 376–382.

3. Hearne, K.M.T. (1982) An Ostensible Precognition of the Accidental Sinking of *HM Submarine 'Artemis'* in 1971. *J.S.P.R.*, 51 (791): 283–287.

4. Hearne, K.M.T. (1982) An Ostensible Precognition of the 1974 Flixborough Disaster. *J.S.P.R.*, 51 (790): 210–213.

**Chapter 5**

1. Carington, W. (1940) Experiments on the Paranormal Cognition of Drawings. *Journal of Parapsychology*, 4: 1–129.

2. Soal, S.G. & Bateman, F. (1954) *Modern Experiments in Telepathy*. Faber & Faber Ltd, London.

3. Marwick, B. (1978) The Soal-Goldney Experiments with Basil Shakleton: New Evidence of Data Manipulation. *Procs. S.P.R.*, 56 (211): 250–277.

4. Rhine, J.B. (1964) *Extra-sensory Perception*. Branden, Boston.

5. Ullman, M., Krippner, S., & Vaughan, A. (1973) *Dream Telepathy*. Mac Millan N.Y.

6. Hearne, K.M.T. (1978) *Lucid Dreams: An Electrophysiological and Psychological Study*. Published Ph.D. Thesis. University of Liverpool, May 1978.

7. Hearne, K.M.T. (1981) Control Your Own Dreams *New Scientist*, 91 (1272): 783–785. 24th September.

8. Hearne, K.M.T. (1985) An Ostensible Precognition Using a 'Dream machine'. *J.S.P.R.*, 53 (799): 18–40.

9. Duval, P. & Montredon, E. (1968) ESP Experiments with Mice. *Journal of Parapsychology*, 32: 153–166.

10. Rhine, J.B. (1974) A New Case of Experimenter Unreliability. *Journal of Parapsychology* 38: 218–225.

11. Rhine, L.E. (1954) Frequencies of Types of Experiences in Spontaneous Precognition. *Journal of Parapsychology*, 18: 93–123.

12. Rhine, L.E. (1955) Precognition & Intervention. *Journal of Parapsychology*, 19 (1): 1–34.

13. Ibid: 17.

14. Ibid: 26.

15. Cox, W.E. (1956) Precognition, an Analysis II. *Journal of the American Society for Psychical Research (J.A.S.P.R).*, 50: 99–109.

16. Barker, J.C. (1967) Premonitions of the Aberfan Disaster. *J.S.P.R.*, 44: 169—181.

17. Hearne, K.M.T. (1984) A Survey of Reported Premonitions and Those Who Have Them. *J.S.P.R.*, 52 (796): 261–270.
18. Eysenck, H.J. and Eysenck, S.B.G. (1964) *Eysenck Personality Inventory*. University of London Press.
19. Cox W.E. (1982) An auditory precognition within a radio newscast, *J.S.P.R.*, 51 (792): 378–381.
20. Orme, J.E. (1974) Precognition & Time. *J.S.P.R.*, 47: 351–365.

**Chapter 6**
1. Stevenson, I. (1970) Precognition of disasters. *J.A.S.P.R.*, 64 (2): 187–210.
2. Gurney, E., Myers, F.W., & Podmore, F. (1886) *Phantasms of the Living*. Trübner, London.
3. Tanagras, A. (1949) The Theory of the Psychobolie. *J.A.S.P.R.*, 43: 151–154.
4. Keil, H.H.J., Herbert, B., Ullman, M. and Pratt, J.G. (1976) Directly Observable Voluntary PK Effects. *Procs. S.P.R.*, 56 (210): 197–235.
5. Keil, H.H.J., & Fahler, J. (1975) A strong case for PK involving directly observable movements of objects recorded on cine film. In Morris, J.D., Roll, W.G. & Morris, R.L. (Eds,) *Research in Parapsychology*. Metuchen, N.J. USA, Scarecrow Press. pp. 66–69.
6. Kulagin, V.V. (1971) Nina S. Kulagina. *Journal of Paraphysics* 5: 54–62.
7. Herbert, B. (1973) Spring in Leningrad: Kulagina Revisited. *Parapsychology Review*. 4: 5–10.
8. Schmeidler, G. (1971) Respice, adspice & prospice. *Procs. of the Parapsychological Assoc* 8: 117–145.
9. Feynmann, R.P. (1949) The theory of positrons. *Physical Review*, 76: 749–759.
10. Dobbs, H.A.C. (1965) Time and extra-sensory perception. *Procs. S.P.R.*, 54: 249–361.
11. Roll, W.G. (1957–64) The psi-field. *Procs. of the Parapsychological Association*, 1: 32–65.
12. Saltmarsh, H. (1938) *Foreknowledge*. G. Bell, London.
13. Broad, C.D. (1937) The philosophical implications of precognition. *Procs. of the Aristotelean Society, Supplement*, 16: 229–245.
14. Dunne, J.W. (1927) *An experiment with time*. Faber, London.

15. Jung, C.G. & Pauli, W. (1955) *The interpretation of nature and the psyche: synchronicity; and the influence of archetypal ideas on the scientific theories of Kepler.* Pantheon, N.Y.
16. Myers, F.W.H. (1903/54) *Human personality and its survival of bodily death.* Longmans, Green, N.Y.
17. Tyrrell, G.N.M. (1953) *Apparitions.* Duckworth. London.
18. Price, H.H. (1948–49) Psychical research and human personality. *Hibbert Journal,* 47: 105–113.
19. Carington, W. (1949) *Matter, mind & meaning.* Methuen, London.
20. Hearne, K.M.T. (1984) A survey of reported premonitions and those who have them. *J.S.P.R.,* 52 (796): 261–270.

**Chapter 7**
1. Lambert, G.W. (1965) A precognitive dream about a water-spout. *J.S.P.R.* 43 (723):5.
2. Haraldsson, E. (1985) Representative national surveys of psychic phenomena: Iceland, Great Britain, Sweden, USA & Gallup's multinational survey. *J.S.P.R.,* 53 (801): 145–158.
3. Foster, J. (1982) *The Case for Idealism.* Routledge & Kegan Paul, London.
4. Price, H.H. (1949) Psychical research and human personality. *The Hibbert Journal,* 47; 105–113.
5. Ibid: 109.
6. van Eeden, F. (1913) A study of dreams. *Procs. J.S.P.R.,* 26 (47): 431–461.

# Index

Aberfan disaster, 87-9
accident survey, 87
acausal theories, 107-8
*Achille Lauro* fire, 66-8
advantageous premonitions,
   58-61
animal studies, 83-4
*Artemis* sinking, 71-3
Askew, Margaret, 48
assassinations:
   Spencer Perceval, 22-3
   President Kennedy, 33-5
   President Anwar Sadat, 64-5
   President Reagan (attempt),
      65-6
   The Pope (attempt), 69
Aubrey, John, 21-2
auguries, 19
Avins, Sylvia, 36
avoidance, 30, 36-40, 55, 83-6,
   117

backwards causation, 102
Bale, S., 27
Ball, B., 25
Barber, Eileen, 60
Barker, Dr John, 87-9, 135
Bellingham, John, 23
Bender, Robin, 54

Berkeley, Bishop, 121
Bessent, Malcolm, 81
Bolton, Frank, 94
Brennan, Lesley, 74-7
Broad, Prof. C.D., 107, 136
Brown, Dolores, 41-2
Brown, Hilda, 26
Brown, Ruth, 47
Burton, Richard, 104

Cambitsis, Mrs R., 94
card-guessing, 79-80
Carver, Shirley, 26, 32
Catherine de Medici, 20
catoptromancy, 18
cause & effect, 102
certainty (conviction) feeling, 13,
   84-5, 111
Chamberlain, G., 47-8
Charles I., 19, 20
Chauvin, Prof. Remy, 83
Cheetham, E., 19, 134
Chuang Tzu, 121
Clinton, Gwendoline, 47
clocks & watches, 44
coincidences, 98
collected premonitions study,
   68-71
Collingwood, Gwen, 38-9

Collins, Janet, 54-5
Conan Doyle, Sir Arthur, 132
Cooke, M., 28
Coombe, Vivienne, 56
Corica, Betty, 26-7
Cottam, David, 33
Cotton, Susan, 50
Cox, W.E., 87, 94-5, 136
critics, 11-12, 128-31
crystal gazing, 18

Daniel, H., 30-31
Davis, J., 22
Davis, Jean, 25, 29
Dawkins, Elizabeth, 46
de Becker, R., 16, 134
definitions of terms, 12-13
déjà vu, 61-2
determinism, 101
displacement premonitions, 32-3,
    47, 56-7
Ditzel, Judith, 27
divination, 17
divine/demonic influence, 108,
    119
Dobbs, Adrian, 106, 136
Dodds, E.R., 17, 134
Douse, Jennifer, 44
drawing experiment, 79
dream precognition, 81-3
dream machine, 81-3
Ducasse, C.J., 106
Dunkling, V., 45-6
Dunne, J.W., 107, 136
Duval, P. & Montredon, E., 83,
    135

Eddowes, Susan, 49
Edward, Duke of York, 18
Egyptians (ancient), 16
Ellis, M., 32
emotions & premonitions, 127
ESP, 13

Eustace, Sheila, 54
Eysenck Personality Inventory,
    91-2, 127, 136

Fairfield, Peter, 50-51
Fairley, Peter, 87
fatalism, 101
Fenn, Olwyn, 43
Ferdinand, Archduke, 23
Feynmann, Richard, 106, 136
Finch, Paul, 36
Fletcher, K., 42-3
Flixborough explosion, 74-6
Foster, J., 121, 137
Fox, C.R., 23
free-will, 101
functional premonitions, 108-10
Furman, Irene, 61
Furman, Robin, 55

Gagarin, Yuri, 35
Gardner, Bobbi, 43
Garwell, Barbara, 63-71, 113,
    125
Gaskell, K., 49, 51
genetic factors, 89-90, 115
Gill, Mary, 33
Great Dream (illusion), 121-6,
    132-3
Green, Pamela, 82-3
group mind, 108
group-replenishment theory, 109
Gurney, E., Myers, F.W., &
    Podmore, F., 103, 136

Hall, D., 37
Halley, Edmund, 21
Haraldsson, E., 114, 137
Harvey-Plews, Norma, 33-4
Hawthorn, Joan, 38
Hearne, Dr Keith, 63, 68, 71, 75,
    82, 89-94, 134-5, 136, 137
Herbert, B., 105, 136

Herman, E., 32-3
Hill, Jacqueline, 36
history & premonitions, 15-24
Hitler, Adolf, 20
Holland, Sylvia, 55
Holmes, Sherlock, 132
Hopkins, Penny, 40
Hughes, Dorothy, 60
Hull, Margaret, 35
Humber ferry, 13
hydromancy, 18

imagery:
   sleep onset (borderland,
      hypnagogic), 15
   visual (waking), 15
induction of premonitions, 127-8
inference, 97-8
Isacke, Mabel, 51
intervention paradox, 102, 119
intervention (see avoidance)

Jackson, Celia, 51-2
Jackson, E., 56
Jackson, Margaret, 61
Jacobs, Mrs., 57-8
James, William, 106, 108
Johnson, Samuel, 121
Jones, Eryl, 88
Jones, Peter, 43
Joyce, Violet, 59-60
Jung, C.G., 107, 137

Kay, B., 34
Keil, H., 104, 136
Kennedy, President, 33-5
Kenyon, Anne, 60
Kitching, Ann, 42
Kulagina, Nina, 104-5
Kulagin, V.V., 104, 136

Lambert, G.W., 112, 137

Lammiman, Philip, 36-7, 52
Lanyi, Bishop Joseph de, 23
latency (premonition to event),
   113
Lawrence, June, 41
Levy, W.J., 83
Lister, Valerie, 19
Lock, Gillian, 50
Lomax, Patricia, 55
lucid dreaming, 81-3, 122-5

MacDonald, Sandra, 71
Mackender, Margaret, 48
Maginot line, 20
McKellar, Peter, 15, 134
Markwick, Betty, 79, 135
Martin, Jessica, 28
McBride, Mary, 27
Media announcement
   premonitions, 34, 93-5
Meier, N., 36
Mellor, Marie, 59
memory and precognition, 96,
   117
Mills, Kathleen, 30
Morgan, Brenda, 44
Morrisey, Lynne, 56-7
multiple time dimensions, 107
Myers, F.W., 18, 108, 137

Neave, Airey, 36
neutral premonitions, 58
noise phenomena, 43, 44
Nostradamus, 19-21, 117

O'Connor, Marie, 41
Old Testament, 18
omens, 18-19, 126
Orme, J.E., 95-6, 112, 136
Osborne, Annette, 57
Oswald, Lee Harvey, 33

passenger statistics, 87

Pauli, H., 23, 134
Pauli, W., 107
Perceval, Spencer, 22
Pope, The (John-Paul II), 69
pre-disaster syndrome, 88
preferential selection, 68-71, 98-9, 115
premonitions bureau, 89
Price, H.H., 108, 121, 137
prodromic dreams, 17, 99
psi-fields, 106
psi-trons, 106
psychobolie, 104
psycho-kinesis (PK) 104-5
psychosomatic avoidance, 38, 109-10

Randall, K., 53
RNG studies, 80-81
Read, Leslie, 52-3
Reagan, President, 65-6, 113
recurring premonitions, 28, 57
Rhine, J.B., 79, 83, 135
Rhine, L.E., 37-8, 39, 84-6, 134, 135
Richards, Geoffrey, 56
Riley, Cherie, 39-40
Roll, W.G., 106, 136
Routh, Eleanor, 49-50

Sadat assassination, 64-5
Saltmarsh, H., 106, 136
Saxton, D., 42
Schmeidler, Dr Gertrude, 106, 136
Schmidt, Dr Helmut, 80-81
Scott-Clark, Phyllis, 61
scrying, 18, 127
self-fulfilling prophecies, 17, 100
Shackleton, Basil, 79
Shakespeare, William, 121
Sidgwick, H., 22, 134

Simpson, Marion, 34
simultaneous telepathy/clairvoyance, 102-4
Smith, Myrtle, 48
Smith, R., 25-6
Soal, S.G., 79, 135
space-time folds, 106
specious present, 106
Stafford, Guy, 29-30
Stevenson, Dr Ian, 103, 136
Stewart, Dawn, 58
Stewart, Gloria, 79
Stratford, M., 46
sub-atomic particles, 106
Sumner, V., 41
Surya, Lorna, 58
Sutton-Shaw, Anice, 28
Swedenborg, 107
Swedish survey, 114
synchronicity, 107

Tanagras, Dr Angelo, 104, 136
Threadgold, Marion, 31-2, 48, 59
time & precognition, 95-6
Townsend, Susan, 58
types of premonition, 13-15
Tyrell, G.N.M., 108, 137

Ullman, Dr M., 81, 135

van Eeden, F., 123, 137
van Gogh, Vincent, 81
Vasiliev, Leonid, 104
Venn, Beatrice, 59

Wallis, Doreen, 11
Watson, J.B., 130
Whately-Carington, W., 79, 108, 135, 137
Whatnall, Gillian, 60-61
White, Rev Dr Claude, 95
White, Rosemary, 31
Wickham, Jenny, 53

Wilkinson, Kay, 34
Williams, Kathryn, 61-2
wish fulfilment, 17, 100

Wolsey, Cardinal, 19
Wood, Marjorie, 28, 49

*By the same author . . .*

# THE DREAM MACHINE
## Lucid Dreams and How to Control Them

We dream for two hours a night, six years a lifetime, yet how often do we realize it? *The Dream Machine* describes the highly original work of Dr Keith Hearne, researcher into 'lucid' dreams — dreams in which people become aware they are dreaming and are then able to control their dreams by thought. The first person in the world to conduct laboratory research into lucid dreams and obtain signals from sleeping subjects, Dr Hearne used his discoveries to develop the Dream Machine.

As well as relating the events that led to the development of his unique invention, Dr Hearne describes fully the exciting new field of lucid dreaming, emphasizing its importance in dream research. With the help of the Dream Machine, dreams were studied from within rather than relying on vague post-waking reports, enabling the discovery of a number of consistent effects in dreams which provide a sound basis for Dr Hearne's new theory of dreaming. He also explores the great potential of dreams in providing inspiration and material for creative pursuits and, in a more philosophical vein, examines old and new theories of dreaming, wondering if life itself may be a kind of Great Dream . . .